RUDYARD KIPLING

BY THE SAME AUTHOR:

CHARACTER AND MOTIVE IN SHAKESPEARE

EIGHT MODERN WRITERS

Novels

THE GUARDIANS

MARK LAMBERT'S SUPPER

A USE OF RICHES

THE MAN WHO WROTE DETECTIVE STORIES

THE MAN WHO WON THE POOLS

THE LAST TRESILIANS

AN ACRE OF GRASS

THE AYLWINS

RUDYARD KIPLING

by

J. I. M. STEWART

LONDON
VICTOR GOLLANCZ LTD
1966

Printed in Great Britain by
The Camelot Press Ltd., London and Southampton

CONTENTS

PREFACE

After a long period of eclipse, which began many years before his death in 1936, Rudyard Kipling has unmistakably come into his own. Mr. Edmund Wilson's essay, 'The Kipling that Nobody Read', first published in *The Atlantic Monthly* in 1941, although on balance not a sympathetic study, directed attention to the remarkable development of Kipling's art in the later stories. In the same year T. S. Eliot published *A Choice of Kipling's Verse*, with an Introduction which ranged perceptively over both verse and prose. Professor Charles Carrington's *Rudyard Kipling: His Life and Work*, appearing in 1955, afforded for the first time a clear and impressive view of the man behind the books. And in 1951 Dr. J. M. S. Tompkins published *The Art of Rudyard Kipling*, which remains the best and most comprehensive critical exposition of its subject.

I am indebted to all these writers, and more immediately to Professor Bonamy Dobrée, whose early essay in *The Lamp and the Lute* (1929) marked the beginning of radical reappraisal, and whose conversation prompted my own renewed interest in Kipling a number of years ago. Mr. Roger Lancelyn Green, the Honorary Librarian of the Kipling Society, published his *Kipling and the Children* in 1965, just in time for me to benefit from his enthusiastic and scholarly discussion of an important facet of Kipling's genius.

J. I. M. S.

RUDYARD KIPLING

CHAPTER ONE

CHILDHOOD

'OUT OF THE WAY, out of the way, there's an angry Ruddy coming!'

Nearly a hundred years ago these words startled passers-by in the quiet English country town of Bewdley. They were being proclaimed by Rudyard Kipling as he stamped down the street. Although not yet three years old, he was already a formidably aggressive child. His grandfather, to whom he was paying a visit, felt quite ill as a result of his 'screaming tempers', and his Aunt Louisa had to reflect that 'the wretched disturbances one ill-ordered child can make is a lesson for all time to me'.

A yet earlier glimpse of Ruddy shows him 'eating his supper, intently watched by three dogs to which he administers occasional blundering blows with a little whip and much shouting'. That had been back in Bombay, his birthplace, where the sun shone, servants behaved respectfully even to the smallest and youngest *sahib*, and all sorts of interesting creatures might walk or glide or fly into one's nursery. Now he had been brought to England in a dark, cold March, and placed for a short time in the care of relatives who, although well meaning and affectionate, expected children to be seen and not heard. Ruddy, who was boisterous by nature, and disposed ceaselessly to demand information about the world around him, didn't like it at all. Perhaps he stepped up his tantrums on this account. He may also have been upset by the occasion of his mysterious transportation: the arrival of a baby sister—an event which it had been judged prudent in the interest of his mother's health to arrange for in England. When, after a short time, Mrs. Kipling and her two children were able to set out again for India, Ruddy was as relieved as were his grandparents.

On two subsequent occasions—once when still a small boy, and once as a young man—Kipling was to arrive in England from the country of his birth, and each of these occasions brought him severe trial. His parents would have described themselves as 'Anglo-Indians'—which was the term for English people who lived and made their careers in India—and during many of his formative years he was an Anglo-Indian too. Because of this, and although he was to be very passionately an Englishman, England never became quite securely his home. Throughout his life he spent more of his time abroad than was then customary even among the wealthy. As a young married man he made a resolute attempt to settle in the United States of America. And when, in middle age, he wrote of England as 'the most marvellous of all foreign countries that I have ever been in', he was framing a paradox which reflected a real truth about himself.

But if Kipling was never quite simply a native of England he was very much a citizen of Great Britain, and a subject of the Queen-Empress Victoria and the King-Emperors who followed her. He was at once the servant and the prophet of the empire which was to rally round the mother-country in two shattering wars. In the first of these wars his only son was killed; of the second he saw the advancing shadow before he died. It may be that he expected too much of the British Empire, and in consequence suffered a needlessly disillusioned, and even embittered, old age. But so much of his best work is bound up with the theme of empire that it cannot be fairly estimated except in the context of an examination of the imperial idea. Such an examination will be briefly attempted later in this book.

Kipling's father, John Lockwood Kipling, was no sort of imperialist. His ancestors, indeed, may have come to England with the Vikings, but for centuries Kiplings had lived in Yorkshire in more or less humble walks of life. Kipling believed them to have been 'small farmers, bell-founders, clock-makers, and the like'. Rather surprisingly, he took little interest in them.

Lockwood Kipling, the son of a Methodist minister, had his career determined for him by a visit in boyhood to the Great Exhibition held in London in 1851, and housed in the famous Crystal Palace erected for it in Hyde Park. Europe had been passing through a phase of turmoil centred in the many revolutions of 1848, and this exhibition, really a kind of trade fair, was primarily designed to show the industrial and economic strength of Britain in an international setting. But what caught young Lockwood's imagination was the application of the fine arts to modern processes of manufacture. He was himself essentially an artist, but an artist with the temperament of a scholar. When the South Kensington Museum was built out of the profits of the Exhibition he worked upon it as a sculptor; after that he designed pottery; and then, when twenty-eight, he was offered the post of Principal, and Professor of Architectural Sculpture, in an art school just established in Bombay by a cultivated Parsee gentleman, Sir Jamsetjee Jeejeeboy. Perhaps because he was anxious to marry, he accepted at once. Sir Jamsetjee got an excellent bargain. In India, Lockwood Kipling had a distinguished career, and it is plain that he would have been a notable figure in any company. Yet socially he might not have made his way as he did (to the great advantage of his son) but for the personality and talents of his wife. If Rudyard's father was a remarkable man, his mother was a woman more remarkable still.

When working at Burslem in the Potteries, Lockwood Kipling had met a young Methodist minister, himself the son and grandson of Methodist ministers, named Frederic Macdonald. The Macdonalds were of Scottish and Irish extraction, fond of preserving family ties, and most of them of more than average ability. Frederic himself was to become eminent in his calling, and of his five sisters who survived childhood four made notable marriages. Georgina married Edward Burne-Jones, one of the most celebrated painters of the age and the close friend of William Morris. Agnes married Edward Poynter, a painter less significant for the history of English art, but famous in his time, and a President of the Royal Academy. Louisa (who was to find the two-year-old Ruddy such a trial) married a wealthy iron-master, Alfred Baldwin, and became the mother of Stanley Baldwin, a British Prime Minister. It was the eldest daughter, Alice, who appeared to make the least striking match; she was merely carried off by Lockwood Kipling to Sir Jamsetjee's obscure school in Bombay, whereas from the same provincial starting-point her sisters had before them the conquest of one or another sphere of London society. But if we are thus to regard the Macdonald sisters as in competition (which they do not themselves appear much to have done), we may conclude that Alice had the best of it in the end. In India she came to move, along with her husband, in the circle of the Viceroy himself. And if her nephew Stanley became Prime Minister in his middle fifties her son Ruddy was to be acknowledged as a writer of genius when still in his twenty-fifth year.

The most assured fact about Kipling's mother is her possession of a sharp and rapid wit. It is convincingly described by her brother Frederic:

> My sister had the nimblest mind and quickest wits I have ever known. She saw things in a moment, and did not so much reason as pounce upon her conclusions. . . . When she was at her ease and the subject was to her mind she was very brilliant, and her felicities of speech and illuminating epigrams were a delight to us all. . . . Her wit was for the most part humorous and genial, but on occasion it was a weapon of whose keenness of point there could be no doubt, and foolish or mischievous people were made to feel it.

Frederic adds that, in comparison, his brother-in-law's mind moved slowly and cautiously, while being at the same time exceptionally retentive and wide-ranging. 'His curiosity was alive and active. . . . All things interested him.' It may be said that Rudyard drew generously upon the endowments of both his parents. He was not perhaps so witty as his mother, and he certainly lacked his father's wise dispassionateness and exactness of taste. What was entirely his own was an urgent and robust imagination.

After the return to India the little Ruddy spent what he was soon to look back upon as a period of departed bliss—in the cool weather at Bombay, and in the hot at Nassik, the nearest hill station. Several of his short stories present an image of himself at this time: a small boy precociously conscious of his heritage as a 'child of the Dominant Race', admired, imperious, stout-hearted. In the posthumously published and not very informative autobiographical sketch, *Something of Myself* (1937), Kipling recalls glimpses of his life at this time: 'light and colour and golden and purple fruits' in a Bombay market; adventurings into Hindu temples, made possible because he was 'below the age of caste'; being so much in the care of Indian servants that Hindustani was 'the vernacular idiom that one thought and dreamed in'; his mother returning from a dinner-party cancelled because 'the big Lord Sahib'—Lord Mayo—had been 'assassinated by a native'. Or again: 'Far across green spaces round the house was a marvellous place filled with smells of paints and oils, and lumps of clay with which I played.

That was the atelier of my Father's School of Art.' Perhaps that is the most significant recollection of the lot. Beginning at an early age, Kipling must have become progressively conscious of his family's involvement in a literary and artistic world having little connection with the official Anglo-India of soldiers and administrators. One day he was going to write, in a poem called 'The Two-Sided Man':

> Much I owe to the Lands that grew—
> More to the Lives that fed—
> But most to Allah Who gave me two
> Separate sides to my head.

As one grows familiar with his life one comes to know what he meant. But in fact there was always to be tension between the Kipling who was an artist bred among artists and the Kipling who admired above all things men of action—or, better, who reverenced active service in the most substantial sense of the term.

In those days all Anglo-Indians who could afford the expense sent their children home to England at about the age of six. This was less in the interest of education, although that was important, than of hygiene. India was a tropical country with a teeming population and only the most rudimentary sanitation; it could be ravaged by epidemic diseases over which medical science was only beginning to gain some measure of control. To the Kipling children, perhaps because of their mother's uncertain health at the time, the remove came a little earlier than to most. Rudyard was five, and his sister Alice—always known in the family as 'Trix'—not yet three, when their parents brought them home to England by way of the new Suez Canal.* After various visits to relations they took the children to Southsea, on the Hampshire coast, and left them (slipping away, it seems, without attempting explanation) in the care of foster-parents whose name they had come across in a newspaper advertisement, and who proved to have satisfactory 'references'.

This rash proceeding has always been regarded by Kipling's

* In *Something of Myself* Kipling says that the canal was not yet opened, and that 'there was a train across a desert'. But he is confusing this journey to England with the earlier one. *Something of Myself* remained unrevised at the time of his death.

biographers as something of a mystery. In 'Baa Baa, Black Sheep', the harrowing story which Kipling was to base upon this first and longer-enduring of the two grim experiences of his boyhood, the mother of the abandoned children is made to say: 'Oh, how long and long and long the time will be! And we have to leave them among strangers.' But this would appear to have been precisely not the Kiplings' plight. In England, Rudyard and Trix had two grandmothers, and three married aunts all of whom were prospering, and all of whom had children much of an age with their Anglo-Indian cousins. The Macdonalds, moreover, were notable keepers-up of family connections, and it seems strange that they were not approached, or did not respond to approaches, at this juncture. Perhaps they gave too much weight to their memories of the 'angry Ruddy' of three years before. Perhaps Alice Kipling, who was still the sister who appeared to have made the least distinguished marriage, elected for complete independence as a matter of pride.

We must here remember that, even in their own homes, Victorian children of the upper and upper-middle classes were brought up at a much greater remove from their parents than has become customary since. Small children were looked after almost entirely by nurses and governesses, and this created a climate in which it seemed quite natural to many Anglo-Indians to have recourse to foster-parents operating on what may be called a straight commercial basis. And had Mrs. Holloway and her son Harry been as kind to Ruddy as was Captain Holloway until his sudden death, we should not now feel any great puzzle about the Southsea arrangement. It was, at least, expected that the children should go to their relations for holidays, and this came about; throughout the rest of his boyhood the Burne-Joneses in particular provided Rudyard with a periodic haven for which he was to be eternally grateful. Nevertheless, one is left with the impression that the Macdonald sisters, including Alice Kipling herself, had something of the hardness or insensitiveness that can accompany brilliance. It is difficult to find any other explanation of why so much misery went unregarded over the next seven or eight years.

'I lived in that house for close on six years', Kipling wrote of Lorne Lodge, Southsea—and then compressed the essence of his experience there into a single paragraph:

It was an establishment run with the full vigour of the Evangelical as revealed to the Woman. I had never heard of Hell, so I was introduced to it in all its terrors—I and whatever luckless little slavey might be in the house, whom severe rationing had led to steal food. Once I saw the Woman beat such a girl who picked up the kitchen poker and threatened retaliation. Myself I was regularly beaten. The Woman had an only son of twelve or thirteen as religious as she. I was a real joy to him, for when his mother had finished with me for the day he (we slept in the same room) took me on and roasted the other side.

Although the outline of the Southsea story is clear enough we cannot be confident that we possess the truth of it in detail. Of the four main sources available, two are in the form of fiction: 'Baa Baa, Black Sheep', and the first chapter of Kipling's novel, *The Light that Failed* (1890). In these it is reasonable to suppose that there would be some manipulating of fact in the interest of dramatic effect. Of Black Sheep, for example, we are not told that he had the alleviation of visits to kindly relatives, and this suppression of autobiographical truth must represent a deliberate darkening of the picture. The other sources, both purporting to be unequivocally autobiographical, were composed in old age: Kipling's *Something of Myself*, and some late reminiscences by his sister. In both these it is possible that things in the first instance invented by Kipling have, with the passing of the years, imperceptibly gained the status of authentic family history. Thus we are told that Black Sheep is sent through Southsea with a placard reading 'Liar' pinned between his shoulders, and this is reiterated as matter of fact in both *Something of Myself* and Trix's recollections. It is conceivable, however, that Kipling first borrowed it (and, indeed, some other things), consciously or unconsciously, from Dicken's *David Copperfield*, and later forgot, as did his sister, that it had not been an authentic experience. We can arrive at no certain conclusion. Mrs. Holloway (or her disagreeable son) may, after all, have read *David Copperfield*, and drawn happy inspiration from the circumstance that to its hero's back was fixed a placard: '*Take care of him. He bites.*'

Again, in 'Baa Baa, Black Sheep' the climax comes when the

persecuted small boy's sight is discovered to be in danger, as we know Kipling's to have been. The mother, on learning this, comes back from India at once—and when she enters her son's bedroom it is to see him fling up an arm instinctively to ward off the expected blow. In *Something of Myself* Kipling reiterates this as a fact, and does so in a form that makes it his mother's recollection rather than his own: 'She told me afterwards that when she first came up to my room to kiss me good-night, I flung up an arm to guard off the cuff that I had been trained to expect.' If this is history uncontaminated by fiction, the moment must have been for Mrs. Kipling one of sudden and brutal shock. And if it was this, her subsequent relations with Mrs. Holloway are difficult to explain. She removed her son from Lorne Lodge, but left her daughter there for a further term of years. Trix's experience had, indeed, been different from her brother's, since Mrs. Holloway appears to have formed for her a genuine affection, which the small girl reciprocated—with the result that she became a precocious little Evangelical herself. At the same time she was obstinately loyal to a brother who was constantly being exhibited to her not merely as the Black Sheep of his family, but veritably as among the damned. The strain upon Trix must have been very great, and leaving her with Mrs. Holloway was, upon any possible reading of the total situation, a grave error of judgement. It comes as no surprise when we learn that in later life Trix was subject to recurrent nervous illness.

But what was the long-term effect upon Kipling himself of his six-years' sojourn in the House of Desolation? One notices how, again and again in the narrative, Mrs. Holloway (whom he was required to call 'Aunty Rosa') is 'the Woman'. There is something savage about the capital 'W', and it seems likely that a fear and dislike of women which Kipling was to betray from time to time took its origin from Lorne Lodge. But Kipling himself answers our question—or rather offers two answers. In the last paragraph of 'Baa Baa, Black Sheep' he writes: 'When young lips have drunk deep of the bitter waters of Hate, Suspicion, and Despair, all the Love in the world will not wholly take away that knowledge.' And in *Something of Myself*, after telling the story of the 'Liar' placard, he says: 'In the long run these things, and many more of the like, drained me of any capacity for real, personal hate for the rest of my days.' These are complementary statements. Kipling did well to acknowledge to himself that the experience of the House of Desolation cast an enduring shadow upon his thought, so that his subsequent view of life, although it was to be manly, acceptive, and capable of a joyous response to many things, was yet fundamentally sombre—as sombre, in essence, as was the vision of his great elder contemporary among English writers, the poet and novelist Thomas Hardy. And while it cannot be said (as it might perhaps be said of Hardy) that the passion of hate was very little known to him, he yet hated individuals, on the whole, only on account of evil general principles for which, in his opinion, they stood. This did not exempt him from certain perils of the spirit. Another of his great contemporaries, the Irish poet W. B. Yeats, wrote in 'A Prayer for my Daughter':

> An intellectual hatred is the worst,
> So let her think opinions are accursed.

There were to be times when 'intellectual hatred' was to betray Kipling into intemperate thought and speech. And he already knew a lot about cruelty; its fearful voice had been all around him, and had inevitably found an echo in his own heart. But he always hated it, and this is the true reason why, being an artist compelled to confront and express all that was urgent in his experience, he was often to admit it to his work.

CHAPTER TWO

SCHOOLDAYS

KIPLING WAS REMOVED from Lorne Lodge in March 1877. He entered the United Services College—a school presently to be described—on 16th January 1878, a fortnight after his twelfth birthday. The intervening nine months appear to have been blissfully happy.

> I was taken at once from the House of Desolation, and for months ran wild in a little farm-house on the edge of Epping Forest, where I was not encouraged to refer to my guilty past. Except for my spectacles, which were uncommon in those days, I was completely happy with my mother and the local society, which included for me a gipsy of the name of Saville, who told me tales of selling horses to the ignorant; the farmer's wife; her niece Patty who turned a kind blind eye to our raids into the dairy; the postman; and the farm-boys. . . . A cousin, afterwards to be a Prime Minister, would come down on visits.

As Stanley Baldwin was two years younger than himself, Ruddy had the satisfaction of becoming a leader in mischief—and to such excellent effect that the farmer declared the boys did each other 'no good'. But now youthful pranks brought no vicious punishment. Nor, what was even more important, was a ceaseless questioning of experience any longer regarded as reprehensible in a small boy. He found out how the windmill worked, and thought to improve Mr. Dally's farming methods by 'teaching one of his cows to stand and be milked in the field'; he fought a successful campaign against a nest of wasps; his mother had to draw a line at his 'return to meals red-booted from assisting at the slaughter of swine'. It was at this time, Trix tells us, that his imagination began to expand, and he would launch into extempore story-telling which took Dally's Farm as a starting-point and then wandered into more romantic worlds.

After Epping Forest came London, where Mrs. Kipling

and her children 'stayed for some weeks in a tiny lodging-house in the semi-rural Brompton Road, kept by an ivory-faced, lordly-whiskered ex-butler and his patient wife'. There were no farm animals here, but at least there were cats on the roofs, and Ruddy and Trix fished for them with cat's-meat at the end of a long string. The ex-butler cannot have approved, and Mrs. Kipling created a diversion by getting her children season tickets for the Kensington Museum across the road. This appears to have been a minor landmark in Rudyard's life. He knew that, in Lahore back in India, his father was now the Curator of a Museum, and he would have been the more curious on that account. He and Trix were so regular in their attendance that they gained a position of privilege, being allowed even into the places marked 'private' where fresh treasures were always being unpacked. There was a big Buddha with a little door in his back, and a great deal else as well:

> There were instruments of music inlaid with lapis, beryl and ivories; glorious gold-fretted spinets and clavichords; the bowels of the great Glastonbury clock; mechanical models; steel- and silver-butted pistols, daggers and arquebusses—the labels alone were an education; a collection of precious stones and rings—we quarrelled over those—and a big bluish book which was the manuscript of one of Dickens' novels. That man seemed to me to have written very carelessly; leaving out lots which he had to squeeze in between the lines afterwards.

Whether Dickens was careless or not, Rudyard was already reading him, and almost anything else he could lay his hands on: exciting novels by Dickens's friend Wilkie Collins, Bret Harte's stories, Emerson's poems; and he used to learn verse by heart for the pleasure of repeating it to himself in bed. And now he was himself a writer as well: 'I had found out, too, that one could take pen and set down what one thought, and that nobody accused one of "showing off" by so doing.'

In 'Baa Baa, Black Sheep' (*Wee Willie Winkie*, 1888) Black Sheep is sent to a day-school along with his tormentor Harry, and dislikes the boys he finds there: 'some of them were unclean, some of them talked in dialect, many dropped their h's.' Black Sheep is so offended by this that he takes courage to denounce the place to Aunty Rosa:

> 'If I was with my father,' said Black Sheep, stung to the quick, 'I shouldn't *speak* to those boys. He wouldn't let me. They live in shops. I saw them go into shops—where their fathers live and sell things.'

Remembering what fun Ruddy was going to have with farm-boys and Saville the gipsy, we may find this a surprising piece of class-prejudice. But Black Sheep is almost certainly not misrepresenting his father—or Ruddy's father. The Kiplings would take it for granted that, if they could possibly afford it, their son should be educated among the sons of gentlemen at a public school. But they were poor, and had to look for something which is really a contradiction in terms: a *cheap* public school. It was a stiff problem—but one which appeared to be solved for them in an almost miraculous fashion.

In the middle of the nineteenth century there had begun an immensely significant reform in the manner of qualifying for the public services of the country. Hitherto, appointments in these services had been largely a matter of influence and family connection, but now they were made to depend upon competitive examinations. The Indian Civil Service led the way in 1855, ten years before Kipling's birth. Then in two crucial years, 1870 and 1871, a Liberal Government under Gladstone applied the same principle first to the Home Civil Service, and then to the Army (in which it had hitherto been possible simply to buy a commission).

These measures are not to be thought of as a head-on attack upon privilege, for the examinations were based upon the curricula followed, or professedly followed, chiefly in the public schools. Many of these ancient establishments, however, were slow to address themselves effectively to the new situation, and this is one reason why numerous new public schools came into existence in the second half of the century. A slightly older school, Haileybury, had been founded in 1805 by what was then the East India Company for their Civil Service students, and here there was a flourishing 'Modern side', including an 'Army class'. And now, in 1874, an offshoot of Haileybury had been set up at Bideford Bay in a remote part of Devon. It was to be a Haileybury at cut prices, and to cater largely for the sons of Army officers, many of them serving in India. The headmaster was Cormell Price, who had organized Haileybury's 'Modern side'. He had brought with him a nucleus of boys from Haileybury itself.

This, then, was the United Services College. The fees were to be kept low by various measures of economy, chief among them being the premises occupied. Somebody had tried to start a holiday resort in Bideford Bay, and had named it Westward Ho! after the popular novel by Charles Kingsley. In spite of this enterprising idea the venture failed to flourish, with the result that there was left high and dry, perched above the sea and with a wilderness of scrub and furze and sandhills behind, a terrace block of twelve large lodging-houses. These were secured, and a covered way was run along the front; attics were knocked together to form dormitories, with locked doors between the 'houses' (in the boarding-school sense of the word), but otherwise doorless and uncurtained; a large hall was added at one end and was known as the gymnasium, although it also served for assemblies, daily prayers, and indoor exercise—including (if *Stalky & Co.* is to be trusted) gigantic public beatings. Under these Spartan conditions Westward Ho! housed, at its point of maximum expansion, something over 200 boys, varying in age between eleven and nineteen.

Not all English public schools are venerably beautiful. On the other hand, none other was quite like this, and the Kiplings might have hesitated to commit their son to the place but for one conclusive factor. They knew Cormell Price—by reputation as a successful schoolmaster, and personally as the valued friend of many of the first writers and artists of the day: Swinburne, William Morris, Dante Gabriel Rossetti. He belonged, in fact, to what was the Kiplings' own circle whenever they were in England. He had already become 'Uncle Crom' to Rudyard, and 'Uncle Crom' he was to continue to be whenever the school holidays began.

Price was clearly a man who impressed himself upon all with whom he came in contact. Kipling in later life was to give to his old school an affectionate regard in which honourable loyalty and the artist's myth-making impulse each had a part. He was to be capable of describing it in a public speech as 'the best school in England', and the section devoted to it in *Something of Myself* is absurdly and rather splendidly headed 'The School before its Time'. In fact the place was to decline when the more securely established public schools took the measure of their new job and got down to it.

In *Stalky & Co.* (1899), as we shall see, Kipling was to paint the United Services College larger than life, and its headmaster (oddly transformed) as larger still. There can be no doubt of the genuineness and strength of his admiration for Price. It appears not only in the Stalky stories but also in an account of the school which he contributed to an American magazine, *The Youth's Companion*, some years before the Stalky saga was launched. This is an important document, and for an obvious reason. We have seen that it is difficult to arrive at the unadorned truth about the House of Desolation simply because it *is* the House of Desolation; because Kipling's powerful imagination, that is to say, hangs like a sombre curtain between us and the facts of the case. And this remains true even when we turn to what other people offer as independent testimony: Kipling has been at work on them to a greater extent than they realize. It is just the same with Westward Ho! Those who knew the school in Kipling's time and have attempted a record of it, all to some extent see it as it has been transformed by Kipling himself. The school as it really existed has been pervasively coloured by his imagination; as a problem for the historian or biographer, indeed, we must admit it to be what Beetle is fond of calling 'metagrobolized'—rendered thoroughly puzzling.

We can be certain, for a start, that Cormell Price had taken on a stiff assignment. We do not know precisely what sort of boys he brought from Haileybury, but it is reasonable to guess that they were a kind whose only chance of scrambling through the not very taxing 'Army Exam' was to cling to this expert teacher. And, after these, Price had to take what boys he could get; it was like recruiting for the French Foreign Legion; no inconvenient questions were asked. In 'An English School', which is the title of the article in *The Youth's Companion*, Kipling puts this in his own way:

> The boys said that those with whom Cheltenham could do nothing, whom Sherborne found too tough, and whom even

Marlborough had politely asked to leave, had been sent to the School at the beginning of things and turned into men. They were, perhaps, a shade rough sometimes.

This last sentence carries an irony of understatement of which the innocent first readers of this account of 'an English school' would be blessedly unaware. For here is another certainty. The United Services College got going—four years before Rudyard's arrival there—to the accompaniment of a quite unusual degree of bullying and brutality among the boys.

This is itself a puzzle. Price was by no means an amateur, but already a public-school master of eleven years' standing. He must have been aware that he was being obliged to accept at least a substantial minority of unreliable and even undesirable boys, and that the masters were not all such as he would have cared to recruit had his resources been less limited. One would expect that he would be on the look-out for trouble, and aware —as Kipling's biographer, Professor Carrington, discreetly puts it—that 'the traditional rules of conduct which stabilize school life and which give a sense of security, even if they are felt to be constricting, had not crystallized'. Price at least had the advantage of starting with moderate numbers, which should have enabled him to ensure that the smaller boys did not have altogether too rough a time. Of course we have to remember that when Rudyard arrived these small boys had become big boys, and they would be likely to mingle any bullying of their own with exaggerated and horrific accounts of what they had themselves endured. Again, the *ethos* of the whole English public-school system was (as, to a varying extent, it remains) pretty tough, and schools far more famous than Westward Ho! have at least lurid patches in their history. But it remains true that, in this important particular, Westward Ho! began very badly, and had improved only a little, if at all, in Rudyard's time. Price, therefore, must either have been an incompetent headmaster or have conducted himself in terms of what most people would now regard as a perverse theory of moral education. In *Stalky & Co.* he comes to us only through a haze of fantasy as the Proosian Bates, who is a kind of Jehovah-figure, illimitably beneficent and wise, yet dealing out punishments the justice of which can be discerned only by the eye of faith (which Stalky and his friends always manage to bring to bear).

Behind this image we descry—but very uncertainly—an actual headmaster who believes that the universe is cruel and senseless, that men must learn to endure it, and that they may as well begin that learning at school.

Rudyard had certainly so begun. Or rather, he had resumed his Southsea lessons. For if we are to realize the full extent of his ordeal we must recall this: that his childhood had been miserable since almost as far back as he could remember; that there had come, from March to December 1877, a brief, delusive interval in which the world seemed a happy place, after all; and that now he was back on Square One, with cruelty and regardlessness seemingly all around him. His nerve broke. 'For the first month or so,' Trix records, 'he wrote to us, twice or thrice daily (and my mother cried bitterly over the letters) that he could neither eat nor sleep.' Is this conceivably another misleading echo from *Stalky & Co.* itself? At first it seems as if it might be so:

> 'Yah!' said Beetle. 'They never really bully—"Molly" Fairburn didn't. Only knock 'em about a little bit. That's what they say. Only kick their souls out of 'em, and they go and blub in the box-rooms. Shove their heads into the ulsters an' blub. Write home three times a day—yes, you brute, I've done that—askin' to be taken away.'

But lately there has come to light a letter written by Mrs. Kipling to Cormell Price on 24th January 1878. It must have been despatched just a little over a week after Rudyard entered the school:

> This morning I had no letter from Ruddy—yesterday I had four. It is the roughness of the lads he seems to feel most—he doesn't grumble to me, but he is lonely and down.

There can be little doubt that 'he doesn't grumble to me' represents Alice Kipling's rather pathetic care not to alienate the headmaster who was also 'Uncle Crom'. She went in tears to her sister, Georgiana Burne-Jones, who responded as almost every experienced mother of an English public-school boy would have done; her own son Philip, she said, had written exactly the same sort of letter when first sent to Marlborough, but he was now very happy there. Mrs. Kipling had to be content with this.

But now comes another puzzle. Mrs. Kipling was still in England—indeed she remained there until October 1880—and one would suppose her to look forward eagerly to the Easter holidays, when Ruddy could join her and she could satisfy herself that things were not too bad. But when the holidays came Lockwood Kipling was on his way home from India, and his wife went to Italy to join him; she had persuaded herself, it seems, that Ruddy had 'quite settled down'. So, with other boys whose parents were far away, or who were reading for Army examinations, he was left to spend the holidays at school. For some reason which seems to have passed unchronicled, he was not able to go to one of his aunts. The ladies may have reflected that Price himself was an honorary 'uncle', after all.

It is impossible not to feel, once more, the hardness of the Macdonalds in this. But Mrs. Kipling need not be convicted of actual heartlessness. It is highly probable that she received assurances from Price that conditions at Westward Ho! would change for the better during the holidays. This turned out to be true. Price himself did become an 'uncle' again, and—what was even more important—such of the terrible bigger boys as also remained turned themselves into tolerant elder brothers. This last circumstance will scarcely surprise anybody acquainted with boarding-schools. Moreover, there may well have been another alleviation. Both in his first term and for a good many terms thereafter, Rudyard had to reckon not only with bullies among his school-mates but with particular ill-treatment by the school chaplain, who was also his first house-master. This man, the Rev. J. C. Campbell, was to draw from Kipling's friend Dunsterville (a level-headed witness) the comment: 'I can never recall his face without an expression of ferocity on it, nor his hand without a cane in it.' During these holidays Campbell probably took himself off to pray and preach elsewhere. He was an emotional preacher, and when he left Westward Ho! after a characteristic performance in the pulpit the boys decided that he ought to be forgiven and offered some parting token of esteem. It was to be Rudyard who cut through such unwholesome benevolence. 'Two years' bullying,' he told his fellows, 'is not paid for with half an hour's blubbering in a pulpit.' This is the voice of maturity, and it tells us of something that was on Rudyard's side. Both physically and intellectually, he grew into manhood very early. (There are photographs of him in his last year at Westward Ho! which suggest a middle-aged man in a schoolboy's fancy dress.)

Price at least seems to have decided against another chaplain of Campbell's stamp, and he introduced in his place the Rev. C. Willes, an easy-going, pipe-smoking character in the tradition of Charles Kingsley's 'muscular Christianity'. Willes lived on friendly terms with the boys, seems to have concerned himself very little with his pastoral function, and is sympathetically presented in *Stalky & Co.* under the name of Gillett. It is worth remarking that Westward Ho! was much more secular in tone than were most public schools of its time, the headmasters of which were themselves Anglican priests more often than not. The grown-up Kipling was to approve of this, and declare that one secret of Price's great hold over his boys lay in the fact that he was not a clergyman. Boys think poorly, he said, of masters who alternate sermons and floggings.

Nearly all the famous English school stories take a system of Draconian corporal punishment for granted. And Kipling could certainly claim to be a well-seasoned product of it:

Western wind and open surge
Took us from our mothers;
Flung us on a naked shore
(Twelve bleak houses by the shore!
Seven summers by the shore!)
'Mid two hundred brothers.

There we met with famous men
Set in office o'er us;
And they beat on us with rods—
Faithfully with many rods—
Daily beat on us with rods,
For the love they bore us.

These stanzas come from a poem set at the beginning of *Stalky & Co.* It is stiff with doctrine—and at the same time certainly the best school song (for it is a kind of school song) ever to have been composed in England:

This we learned from famous men,
   Knowing not its uses,
When they showed, in daily work,
Man must finish off his work—
Right or wrong, his daily work—
   And without excuses.

Kipling was never to make friends easily—nor, it seems, much to feel the need of them; in his writings the strongest bonds between man and man are those celebrated here: daily work and duty. Any warmth of affection in him instinctively confined itself within a family circle. His most intimate schoolfellows, George Beresford and Lionel Dunsterville, are perhaps best described as cronies. They were to become M'Turk and 'Stalky' Cockran: with himself as 'Beetle', the joint heroes of an immortal book. There is some uncertainty as to just when the three boys formed a close association. Kipling seems first to have teamed up with Beresford, an Irish boy, aloof in manner and sharp of tongue, who had already been at Westward Ho! for a year. Dunsterville, although about the same age as the others, had arrived a year earlier still, and had thus suffered the full horrors of the school's earliest phase. He was a soldier's son, but with an unhappy home background; he tended to be solitary, and to get satisfaction out of harassing those set in authority over him; he had a talent for small practical jokes so perpetrated that he himself remained invisible; and it was this special endowment which he brought to the confederacy when he joined it. Kipling tells us that 'stalky' in the school's vocabulary meant 'clever, well-considered and wily, as applied to plans of action'. It is perhaps significant that the historical Dunsterville did *not* have the nickname 'Stalky' while at Westward Ho! The three friends did, no doubt, indulge in the sort of escapades which were to be so gloriously magnified in *Stalky & Co*. At the same time, they appear to have been rebels only against the minor conventions of the place, and the other boys may well have viewed them more as the intellectuals and aesthetes of the school than as the boisterous anarchists we know in the stories.

It is clear, too, that Kipling never really fell out of grace with his headmaster. All three boys, indeed, had interests which would commend them to Cormell Price. English Army officers then were not characteristically men of any very wide culture, and a school in which there was a heavy concentration of their sons was bound to be preponderantly 'philistine' in tone. Price, with his background in Pre-Raphaelitism and his literary and artistic friends, can never really have felt wholly at home in it, so boys who read Ruskin and Carlyle, decorated their bleak little study after the approved aesthetic fashion of the day, and adorned it with blue-and-white china and scraps of mediaeval wood-carving, cannot have been other than interesting to him. Within a few months of Rudyard's entering the school Lockwood Kipling had written to Price in an apologetic and almost disparaging way about his son as 'a desultory soul' who would 'always be inclined to shirk the collar and to interest himself in out of the way things'. But it is evident that while Rudyard's father saw his future as that of a journalist (which, in fact, it was to be for a number of years) Price from quite early on believed that he would be a creative writer, and took care to foster the boy's ability in various ingenious ways.

Here, perhaps, is the real basis of Kipling's enduring regard for Price. It was not that Price possessed (what Bates is credited with in the stories) monumental wisdom and a deep understanding of boyhood. Many Victorian headmasters have been so represented, alike in biography and in fiction. This was a convention of the time, and Bates is adorned with it—as well as with an equally conventional zeal in beating his pupils, an activity which Price appears to have been content to leave mainly to others. The true bond lay in the fact that Price and Kipling were in much the same boat. Through all his formative years, Kipling was to be poised between two worlds: a world in which literature and the arts were regarded as among the most serious things in life, and a world of soldiers and administrators—men of action, prone to regard artists and writers as unreliable characters, disagreeably tricked out with long hair and velvet jackets. Kipling's actual career was to be a triumph over the difficulties of this divided loyalty, since he was to become the greatest of all English writers dedicated to celebrating the life of action.

During his later years at school it became evident to his two friends that he had a foot in another world than Westward Ho! At the end of his first summer term he had gone to Paris with his father, who was arranging the Indian section of the Exposition there, and he had been allowed to roam the city at will; he seems to have formed, there and then, that love of France which his subsequent aggressive British patriotism was never to impair. His reading, moreover, could not but reveal itself to his school-fellows as exceptionally wide—and also as mysteriously directed, for how could he have found his way not merely through the English classics from Bunyan and Defoe to Landor and Browning, but also to so much contemporary American writing: Emerson and Longfellow, Poe and Whitman, as well as Bret Harte and Mark Twain and the magnificent and brand-new *Uncle Remus*? All this, and the fact that he was himself constantly scribbling both verse and prose, Rudyard could not, of course, conceal. But he was wary about admitting to his family connections; his holidays were shrouded in secrecy; even Beresford knew nothing of the brilliant aunts and eminent uncles until after leaving school.

The three boys who moved up together from form to form, always in close confederacy (and always cunningly sharing out their 'prep' on co-operative principles), were popular neither with the boys at large nor with the majority of the masters—by whom they were regarded as minor rebels and chronic nuisances. Rudyard, who had arrived as an unmuscular child, at a disadvantage both in fisticuffs and in games because of his defective vision (and looking rather like a 'cave-boy', Beresford records), found that strength came to him suddenly towards the end of his second year. This, and his increasing seniority, meant an end of bullying, and there is every evidence that he ended by conquering the United Services College and enjoying its graceless but rugged life hugely. He may even have been disconcerted when he was suddenly taken away from it—some months before his seventeenth birthday, and thus a year or thereabouts earlier than the customary age for leaving a public school.

If, at the time of choosing a school for their son, Lockwood and Alice Kipling had shown much more foresight than parents commonly manage, they might have seen that there was a real snag about Westward Ho! The school had been invented to get boys into the Army, but there was no future in the Army for one who, without spectacles, saw as a mere blur anything more than a few yards from his nose. Kipling was never to regard himself, or to be regarded, as an 'intellectual'. (Indeed, he was to denounce intellectuals in one of his poems as 'brittle' creatures, who 'crack beneath a strain'.) But from the first it must have been apparent that he was an exceptionally intelligent boy. For such boys, Oxford or Cambridge was a natural goal. But the teaching at Westward Ho! was not in the least adapted to preparing a boy to gain a scholarship at a university, nor was there among the boys the particular sort of competitive spirit that gets a scholarship candidate along. On the other hand, the Kiplings could not afford to enter Rudyard as a commoner at an Oxford or Cambridge college. So Lockwood Kipling tackled his son's vocational problem as well as he could—and having particularly in mind the fact that the boy scribbled the most admirable letters home. As a result, Rudyard appears simply to have been summoned by Price one day and told that, a couple of weeks after the end of term, he was to return to India, where a job on a newspaper had been found for him at a salary of 100 silver rupees a month.

In *Stalky & Co.* Beetle is represented as rushing in upon his friends with his news in a state of wild jubilation. But it is not certain that Rudyard really felt like that at the time. He was sophisticated enough to know the advantages of a fully academic education. 'My salaams to Stanley [Baldwin],' he was to write from India two years later. 'I'd give something to be in the Sixth at Harrow as he is, with a University Education to follow.' And now, in what had suddenly become his last few weeks at school, there was probably another consideration in his mind. Just as he knew that a schoolboy must conquer Westward Ho! he knew that a writer must conquer the literary world of London. He already had a toe-hold there, since he was known to people powerful in that world as a youth of brilliant promise. To return to India was, indeed, to return to his parents, whom he deeply loved. But it was to be sent into exile, all the same.

And there was something more—something which takes us straight back, strangely enough, to the House of Desolation. In 1880, when he was fourteen-and-a-half years old, Rudyard went to Southsea to collect Trix, who was still in the care of Mrs. Holloway. This renewed encounter with 'Aunty Rosa' is an incident we should like to have a record of. But we do know about something else that happened. There was now a new boarder at Lorne Lodge, 'a straight slender girl with a beautiful ivory-pale face and a cloud of dark hair'. Her name was Florence Garrard; she was a little more than a year older than Rudyard; and Rudyard fell in love with her.

We have to remember how physically precocious he was; it is recorded that when he first arrived at Westward Ho! his upper lip already showed the ghost of a moustache. In the simplest sense, then, there was some basis in maturity to this boy-and-girl affair. And, of course, its psychological background is curious. Florence's beauty was of a type which Rudyard had been taught to admire in the paintings of the Pre-Raphaelites—and she was in thrall to the dragon of Lorne Lodge! This was sufficient ground in itself to add romantic feeling to a first upsurge of physical attraction. What is extraordinary is that Rudyard continued to contrive meetings with the girl throughout the rest of his schooldays. And when he sailed for India, some three months before his seventeenth birthday, he believed himself to be engaged to her. In point of fact, it was to be only by accident that they ever met again. We know little about Florence Garrard. But she was to be the girl in Kipling's strange and painful autobiographical novel, *The Light that Failed.* And his Aunt Edith (the unmarried Macdonald sister) was to recall 'how impressed she had been by the alarming force of his feelings as he gave her an account of his love for Flo Garrard, the girl who took his heart when he was still a schoolboy and did it no good before she tossed it back to him'.

CHAPTER THREE

INDIAN YEARS

THE RUDYARD KIPLING who set sail from England in September 1882 was still a schoolboy alike in years and in much of his behaviour. He was noisy, talkative, inquisitive, and largely given to pranks and inordinate laughter. But along with this went two things: the generous admixture of emotional precosity which had made Flo Garrard so important to him when so young, and the habit of constant association with artists and writers. 'All the people one was taken to see either wrote or painted pictures', he records—and adds as an afterthought: 'or, as in the case of a Mr. and Miss de Morgan, ornamented tiles.' During his schooling, holidays not spent with the Burne-Joneses or the Poynters were passed in the care of three sisters who 'took charge of schoolgirls and young students'; and these ladies had known Carlyle and were themselves much immersed in literary pursuits and literary society. They must have looked forward to Rudyard's becoming a writer. And so, too, must his parents out in India. One of his first discoveries when he arrived there was that, without letting him know, they had caused to be printed for private circulation a number of his poems, under the title of *Schoolboy Lyrics* (1881). He is said to have sulked for three days when this was divulged to him; and no doubt both the venture and the title chosen for it are good examples of the inept kind of thing that admiring parents can do. But at least we see that Lockwood and Alice Kipling had hopes for him extending beyond a newspaper office.

During the voyage out, however, it is likely that his thoughts were about something quite different from authorship. For in its long passage from Tilbury to Bombay, the liner *Brindisi* was going to pass through a theatre of war. This brings us straight to the theme of empire.

To the north-west of India lay Afghanistan, a vast mountainous territory dominated by martial tribes not very different from those which Alexander the Great had encountered there three hundred years before the birth of Christ. Beyond Afghanistan in turn lay imperial Russia—the growing power and expansionist policy of which constituted the principal anxiety of the British Government in India. In a costly and largely futile campaign fought in 1878–1880, an army under General Roberts had first invaded and then evacuated Afghanistan, and a succession of small frontier wars was to follow. But now the centre of anxiety was Egypt, and what lay at stake (as several times since) was the control of the Suez Canal. Under Arabi Pasha, a nationalist revolt had broken out against the international commission then controlling the country. There were French and British fleets in the harbour of Alexandria; when Arabi mounted batteries against them, the French hesitated; meanwhile, there were massacres in Cairo, and the British Consul had been attacked. The British Prime Minister, Mr. Gladstone, ordered the bombardment of Arabi's fortifications, and this was effectively carried out on 11th July 1882. Then a British Army was landed, commanded by Sir Garnet Wolseley and including the Brigade of Guards. They seized the Canal, and after a short and brilliant campaign Arabi was completely defeated at Tel-el-Kebir.

Great Britain was ringing with the news of this victory in the very week that Kipling set sail. The *Brindisi* was held up for four days at Port Said before venturing through the Canal, and meanwhile the battlefield ('strewn with unburied corpses', as Mr. Carrington says) lay only fifty miles away. It is unlikely that even so enterprising a boy as Rudyard got near it—particularly as we can be fairly sure that somebody had been told off to keep an eye on him during the voyage. But he had just come from years of close association with youths whose family tradition must have made them burn to be serving under Wolseley, and he himself must have been enormously excited. Certainly during these few days he took as firm and tenacious a grip of Port Said and Suez in imagination as the soldiers of Queen Victoria were taking in fact. And now, beyond the stretching desert, through the Gulf of Aden, across the Arabian Sea, lay what made the British occupation of Egypt a strategic necessity: the Empire of India. So much of Kipling's genius is bound up with this strange and rather impressive historical phenomenon that some brief account of its character, and the manner of its coming into being, is here essential.

India is well accustomed to armies of occupation. Its history, for untold centuries before European nations began to establish trading-posts there, is one of successive waves of conquest pouring in from the north—and largely by the same route along which Kipling's contemporaries were to fear that the Russians might advance. If India can be said to have had a golden age, this lay in the period of Gupta rule in the fourth and fifth centuries of our era; it ended with a great invasion by the Huns from Central Asia; and soon after that came the first of a long series of onslaughts by Mohammedan armies. The indigenous Hindu population, split up under the sovereignty of innumerable petty rajahs, was seldom capable of effective resistance. Some warlike races, indeed, there were; and the Rajputs, Sikhs, and Marathas successively offered sufficient resistance to prevent the greater part of the subcontinent from being wholly submerged beneath Mohammedan beliefs and institutions. But great empires were eventually established by the invaders, and under the Mogul rulers—notably Babur and his grandson Akbar—there were periods of relative stability. The Mogul empire finally disintegrated, and the last great struggle for India was between the Marathas, the Sikhs, and those European powers which had already achieved a footing on Indian soil.

The warfare which had thus for eight or nine centuries ravaged India was warfare, for the most part, of an unbelievable ferocity and ruthlessness. For this the religious fanaticism of Islam was largely responsible. 'The suffering caused in India,' one historian writes, 'by campaigns between A.D. 1000 and A.D. 1859 probably, for a certain wanton and luxurious quality of cruelty, surpassed that endured by all the world besides.'

The first Europeans to present themselves in any number before this spectacle were the Portuguese, who established a 'factory' at Calicut in 1500, and promptly turned upon the Mohammedans a cruelty as abominable as their own. England was later in the field, but in 1600 the East India Company was founded, and given a charter by Queen Elizabeth the First. It was to be still the supreme British authority in India when Kipling's father was growing into manhood, and in this fact we have an index of the extent to which the Western penetration of India was a matter of mercantile interests. The clash of these led to open if petty warfare between the representatives of one European power and another. The Portuguese, the first to come, were the first to go. The Dutch went too, but maintained a hold on the East Indies. The French did not arrive until 1674, but then remained formidable for nearly a century. After that, Great Britain ruled all India, directly or indirectly, for nearly two hundred years. For long this government was, by good Western standards, venal and corrupt; and it was a regular defence of those charged with misconduct that to get anything done in India one had to do as the Indians did. The argument, although never other than shabby, held a certain validity for as long as the English, in manœuvring for power, had to accommodate themselves to customs and standards not their own. It weakened as their effective control of the country grew. Happily, the East India Company, though not notably progressive, did come to see that its interests would be best pursued by servants who looked to an adequate salary for support and were not expected to subsist on perquisites and bribes. This, and an improved ethic of public service in Great Britain itself, had a progressive effect—as had, too, the introduction of recruitment by examination. In point of personal integrity and devotion to duty the 'Indian Civil' eventually came to rank among the great achievements of the nineteenth century.

But that is not the whole story. In some important regards it is the first, and not the second, half of the nineteenth century that saw what was best of Anglo-India. And even that was no golden age. Much of the spectacle presented by Indian life, whether Mohammedan or Hindu, was unlikely to commend itself to Western observers. The indigenous inhabitants appeared to have little notion of public order, common honesty, sanitation, and numerous other desirable things. Their laws were bewilderingly various, but almost always barbaric and often abominable. Suttee (the custom whereby wives were burnt to death on their husband's funeral pile), female infanticide, mutilation and torture were all prominent upon the scene, and a long period of struggle against such enormities inevitably bred scorn and dislike in the new rulers—who, moreover, being men of action, remained comparatively little aware of the less immediately obvious achievements of Indian civilization. It was natural, too, that the Anglo-Indians should take on something of the authoritarian spirit which lay so heavily over the country already. Nevertheless, between such of the English and Indians as were prompted to it, acquaintance and even intimate friendship was possible, and as a consequence of this the government often showed a reasonable understanding of Indian points of view. Whatever this promised for the future—and it may not have been a great deal—was blotted out in 1857 by the terrible disaster of the Indian Mutiny.

'Mutiny' should perhaps be distinguished as the British word for what happened, since it was, after all, a desperate attempt by those to whom the land belonged by birth to throw off an alien and foreign rule. British stupidity—of a common, soldierly kind—started it; Indian murderousness and cruelty carried it on; British force and ruthlessness had crushed it by 1859—and it was in the interim that the outmoded East India Company passed into limbo and the British Crown took over. There was a moving and unflinching heroism on each side, but the aftermath was bitter indeed. The forces working for a more complete separation between rulers and ruled were now vastly accelerated. India was, once more, a country subjected to conquerors. They were, it is true, a new sort of conqueror. *Parcere subiectis et debellare superbos* . . . they proposed to give the losers a square deal, subject tyranny to the rule of law, and in general put any amount of sweat into the business of making things work. This is what Kipling was to see. But they were also to be as contemptuously aloof towards, and as arbitrarily commanding over, the Queen's Indian subjects as any prefects at Westward Ho! could be in their relations with the lowliest boys beneath them. This, Kipling saw less clearly. India, the land of castes, must itself in some degree be held responsible for creating and acknowledging the caste of the white *sahibs*. Kipling was never to doubt that it existed, and that he believed in it.

His first employment was on a provincial newspaper published in Lahore, the *Civil and Military Gazette*. He was thus able to live with his parents, and this it had perhaps been judged best that a boy not yet past his seventeenth birthday should do. His mother's first action was to insist on his shaving off the 'real whiskers' which set an unnatural emphasis upon his already marked maturity. There is no sign that he resented this prompt tyranny; and of Lockwood and Alice Kipling, now as at all other times, he writes with the warmest affection. 'We delighted more in each other's society than in that of strangers and when my sister came out, a little later, our cup was filled to the brim. Not only were we happy, but we knew it.' The parents and their two children were to speak of themselves as 'the Family Square'. It appears to have been Alice Kipling who invented the expression—the reference being to the famous defensive formation still adopted by British infantry soldiers at the end of the nineteenth century. Four-square, the Kiplings could face up to the world.

This solidarity was for long to mean much to Kipling, for his dazzling precocity was not of a kind urging him to a swift independence of family influence. When he had already begun to make a name for himself as an author, he gave up one particular vein of fiction which his mother judged—correctly enough—to be rather cheaply cynical. His father remained a literary mentor all his days; when writing of any importance was in question, Kipling was always reluctant to send it to the Press until it had been 'smoked by the pater'. He was showing quite as much judgment as filial duty here, since Lockwood Kipling had a more discriminating and exacting taste than his own. Kipling was to remain fairly closely within his family circle throughout his seven years in India; when he left it, as we shall see later, his sense of security was impaired, and so remained until he once more had around him a family of his own.

There was a good deal in his new circumstances to make him feel adequately acknowledged as grown up. He had his own manservant and his own pony-and-trap; as he was the only European on the staff of the *Civil and Military* apart from its editor, he had a certain amount of responsibility as well as a great deal of hard work of a routine and unexciting sort. He was made a member of the Punjab Club, 'where bachelors, for the most part, gathered to eat meals of no merit', and where he was able to listen to endless talk:

> And in that Club and elsewhere I met none except picked men at their definite work—Civilians, Army, Education, Canals, Forestry, Engineering, Irrigation, Railways, Doctors, and Lawyers—samples of each branch and each talking his own shop. It follows then that that 'show of technical knowledge' for which I was blamed later came to me from the horse's mouth, even to boredom.

'Picked men at their definite work': the phrase is quintessential Kipling, covering almost everything he admired and the greater part of what he was to write about.

Yet he was far from confining his interest to the society of his fellow-countrymen. He had no sooner encountered the sights and sounds of Bombay, his birthplace, than the Hindustani which had been virtually his nursery language began to come back to him. In Lahore, after the *Civil and Military* had gone to press, he would wander through the old Moslem city 'in all manner of odd places—liquor-shops, gambling and opium-dens, which are not a bit mysterious, wayside entertainments such as puppet-shows, native dances; or in and about the narrow gullies under the Mosque of Wazir Khan'. Back in the little house in the Brompton Road (where he and Trix had fished for cats), the habit of 'night-waking' had come to him, and he was to know later that, as an artist, his fortunate hour was 'on the turn of sunrise, with a sou'-west breeze afoot'. Now he felt that he had the freedom of all the mysterious East for his nocturnal wanderings.

Although much of his childhood had been unhappy, and a full share of human sorrow was to come to him in manhood, he yet felt, when he came to look back on his life from the viewpoint of his seventieth year, that 'every card in [his] working life had been dealt him in such a manner that [he] had but to play it as it came'. '*Working* life' is perhaps significant in this statement, but it is certainly true that his 'seven years' hard' in India fell out fortunately for his career as a writer. The period began with a straight grind with ink and paper, scissors and paste, that taught him much; and it began, too, with a status that was thoroughly advantageous. A young newspaperman had a very lowly place in the rigid hierarchy of Anglo-Indian society—or rather, a place half out of it. As a *sahib* he was admitted to those clubs in which were congregated all that rank-and-file of administrators and officers who were getting things done, but at the same time there was nothing in his situation to debar him from exploring much humbler regions. He got to know all sorts of 'natives' in a way that must have made him one of the best-informed young men in India. He cultivated the acquaintance not only of the British officers of the Indian Army, but of the British rankers as well; he was to be the first, and with few exceptions the last, author of any eminence to write with knowledge and insight about non-commissioned officers and men.

After his service on the *Civil and Military* at Lahore he was promoted to that of the *Pioneer* at Allahabad, a paper with a nation-wide circulation, and this was a move taking him from Moslem to Hindu India, so that he came to understand both sides in India's perennially tragic conflict. Moreover, at the end of 1884, when he was close on his nineteenth birthday, a change at the very peak of government had an unexpected influence upon his life. Lord Ripon, a serious and reforming Viceroy (who, as a young man, had been a 'muscular Christian', and a friend of Thomas Hughes of *Tom Brown's Schooldays*), retired, and was succeeded by Lord Dufferin, a cultivated man of the world, acceptive of talented and intelligent acquaintance wherever he found it. Lockwood Kipling gave the Dufferins' daughter drawing-lessons; and his wide learning, together with Alice Kipling's charm, resulted in the family becoming accepted members of the viceregal circle on its less formal and official side. When they could afford it, Mrs. Kipling and her daughter began to spend the hot weather at Simla, and Lockwood and his son would join them during periods of leave.

Simla was an astonishing place, and requires brief description. It was one of a number of 'hill stations' on the lower slopes of the Himalaya—villages or small towns in which Europeans found refuge from the torrid heat of the plains in an Indian summer. So precipitous was the terrain upon which it was pitched that, within its quite modest boundaries, one could move from 6,600 to 8,000 feet above sea-level. Here the Viceroy was accustomed to establish his seat of government for half the year, occupying a converted shooting-lodge which Lady Dufferin used to declare was the smallest house she had ever lived in. Here, with a staff consisting of two principal secretaries, a dozen aides-de-camp, and a corps of messengers, the Viceroy administered, virtually with an absolute power, a mingling of races more than twice as numerous, and ten times as densely planted, as the present population of the United States of America. Simla was remote, and by modern standards almost inaccessible, but from all over India princes and governors would be summoned to audience. There can scarcely have been a stranger or more fascinating spectacle in the world—and for a month or two of the year Kipling had the freedom of it. He was proving slow to pick up any social graces. But the Dufferins were aware of him, and of his writing.

Almost inevitably, Simla had a reputation in British India for being 'fast'—a place where morals were undesirably relaxed. Both the Viceroy and the Commander-in-Chief of the Army, who also spent much time in Simla, were surrounded by a large *entourage* of young, unattached Englishmen, most of them of good family and adequate leisure, whose social life largely consisted in flirting with ladies sent to Simla, at once to be fashionable and to escape the heat, by husbands and fathers who were still toiling at their duties through the desperate summer far below. Some of Kipling's early writing takes the form of precociously cynical and 'knowing' sketches of this society. His father seems not to have objected too much, provided the workmanship was good. His mother, who although now a fashionable lady had that strong Methodist ancestry behind her, can be discerned as not too pleased. She need not have worried. Her son's genius was by many times too vigorous and abundant to rest in mere light-hearted chronicles of scandal. For a time—and being, perhaps, rather conscious of family leading-strings—he got satisfaction from building up a small reputation for clever writing of this sort. But his developing bent lay elsewhere, and predominantly in a vigorous and freely imaginative handling of a world in which drawing-rooms and tea-parties were of little importance. Actual incidents and anecdotes, constantly crowding in upon him from the multifarious active life of India, were what provided him with the material for his earliest stories and poems.

CHAPTER FOUR

INDIAN WRITING

KIPLING, WITH HIS seventeenth birthday just behind him, took one look at India—perhaps one sniff as well—and began to write. At the start there was nothing to be done with the stuff except to send it back to Dunsterville, still at Westward Ho!, for publication in the *United Services College Chronicle*. This is the humblest resource of budding authors who have just left school. His first chief on the *Civil and Military Gazette* seems to have felt, reasonably enough, that nothing could be less useful in his only European assistant than undefined literary ambitions, and it was by way of unassuming reporting, first of minor and later of more important public occasions, that Kipling won his own way into the paper's columns. But his talent was far too powerful, and far too prolific, to fail of recognition for long.

First in the *Civil and Military* itself, and then in the more widely circulating *Pioneer*, he was soon writing occasional pieces which could be regarded as either expanded anecdotes or very short stories. The volume which we know as *Plain Tales from the Hills* (1888) is made up of forty of them. Collections of this sort are often not to their writer's advantage, since what may have seemed reasonably diversified and resourceful when read over a period of time in newspapers reveals sameness and repetitiveness when brought together within the covers of a book. But this is not true of *Plain Tales;* one can read the volume through from start to finish and be chiefly impressed by the range and variety of what is presented. Take, for instance, two stories about children. 'Tods' Amendment' is a robust little story concerning a small—a very small—celebrity. 'Every one in Simla knew Tods. Most men had saved him from death on occasions. He was an utterly fearless young Pagan, about six years old, and the only baby who ever broke the holy calm of the Supreme Legislative Council.' The story tells us just how the baby *sahib* achieved this feat, and how the Viceroy and the Commander-in-Chief themselves were obliged to break off their deliberations in order to help Tods catch his pet goat.

Tods, however, does them a useful service in his turn. Because he frequents the Simla Bazaar, he is an authority on 'the real native—not the hybrid, University-trained mule', and so he is able to set the Government of India right in some matter of agrarian reform; a Bill is passed, and it includes 'Tods' Amendment'. Over against this cocky little story of a white child may be set 'The Story of Muhammad Din'—Muhammad Din being a brown child. His father, Imam Din, is the narrator's man-servant, who is scandalised when he finds his son actually playing in his master's dining-room. But the narrator now regards Muhammad Din as an acquaintance, and they greet each other ceremoniously every day:

> Muhammad Din never had any companions. He used to trot about the compound, in and out of the castor-oil bushes, on mysterious errands of his own. One day I stumbled upon some of his handiwork far down the grounds. He had half buried the polo-ball in dust, and stuck six shrivelled old marigold flowers in a circle round it. Outside that circle again was a rude square, traced out in bits of red brick alternating with fragments of broken china; the whole bounded by a little bank of dust. The water-man from the well-curb put in a plea for the small architect, saying that it was only the play of a baby and did not much disfigure my garden.

The narrator unfortunately tramples down this palace in the dark, and a malicious servant tells the little boy that the *sahib* has done this deliberately and in anger. Muhammad is heart-broken, but eventually reassured. He resumes his solitary play:

> A gaily-spotted sea-shell was dropped one day close to the last of his little buildings; and I looked that Muhammad Din should build something more than ordinarily splendid on the strength of it. Nor was I disappointed. He meditated for the better part of an hour, and his crooning rose to a jubilant song. Then he began tracing in the dust. It would certainly be a wondrous palace, this one, for it was two yards long and a yard broad in ground-plan. But the palace was never completed.

The child has fallen ill, and an English doctor is called in and does his best:

> 'They have no stamina, these brats,' said the Doctor, as he left Imam Din's quarters.
>
> A week later, though I would have given much to have avoided it, I met on the road to the Mussulman burying-ground Imam Din, accompanied by one other friend, carrying in his arms, wrapped in a white cloth, all that was left of little Muhammad Din.

This story exhibits one sense in which these 'tales' are 'plain': not (as with many of them) 'robustly outspoken', but 'simple and unadorned'. Kipling has given us a glimpse of the pathetic insecurity of native life—and has done so with the same sort of frugal artistry that Muhammad Din had had to employ in his little buildings.

In contrast with this we might set any of the stories told by, or about, three imaginary private soldiers whom Kipling was to make famous: Mulvaney, Ortheris, and Learoyd (*Soldiers Three*, 1888). Thus in 'The Taking of Lungtungpen' Mulvaney tells of an action against a band of dacoits in Burma. The whereabouts of these robbers is extracted, not gently, from a prisoner, and the British soldiers strip to swim a stream by night, and then enter and capture Lungtungpen armed but stark naked. 'We wint into thim, baynit an' butt, shriekin' wid laughin' '—and a great slaughter of dacoits follows. There are woman and children in Lungtungpen, and their terror is naturally increased by the extraordinary appearance of the attackers. But the soldiers spend the rest of the day playing with the Burmese babies, 'fat little, brown little divils, as pretty as picturs'. At the head of this story, as was to be his frequent habit, Kipling sets an excerpt from one of his own poems:

> So we loosed a bloomin' volley,
> An' we made the beggars cut,
> An' when our pouch was emptied out,
> We used the bloomin' butt,
> Ho! My!
> Don't yer come anigh,

When Tommy is a playin' with the
baynit an' the butt.

This is a very different world of feeling from that of 'The Story of Muhammad Din'. And wholly different again is 'The Gate of the Hundred Sorrows'. Here there is no story, only the ramblings of a mortally stricken opium smoker in Lahore. At school Kipling had been an admirer of Robert Browning's command of the dramatic monologue in verse, and now at eighteen (for this is the earliest written of the *Plain Tales*) he has carried the technique over into prose with an astonishingly precocious artistry. From beginning to end, the texture and cadence of the writing convey, powerfully and precisely, the particular sort of disintegration of personality that opium addiction brings about.

It may be said that by the time he was twenty-one Kipling had written both stories and poems which were to contribute permanently to his fame. And the beginning of fame itself came early, for in 1888, before his twenty-third birthday, an enterprising publisher holding a contract for Indian railway bookstalls started a series to be called the Indian Railway Library, and the first six volumes consisted entirely of short stories by Rudyard Kipling. These not only established his reputation in India; they spread it abroad with surprising rapidity as well. The small and inexpensive volumes were, after all, intended for *travellers*. And travellers, whether to England or to America, finding them still in their trunks when they reached their destination, would hand them over to friends as something rather remarkable. This time, the cards had been dealt to Kipling very luckily indeed.

But there was more than luck, of course, in the success gained by these stories—the immediate successors to *Plain Tales from the Hills*, and now to be found in the volumes *Soldiers Three* and *Wee Willie Winkie*. Not all of them are good, and a few are rather horrid. 'Wee Willie Winkie' itself, and its companion story, 'His Majesty the King', are thickly sentimental presentations of childhood in a manner not at all to our taste today. Kipling was to write with genius for children, but not invariably with genius about them. Some stiffly guarded Victorian conventions and expectations barred the way. Yet in this early collection there are two further stories about children each of which is impressive in its fashion. The first, 'Baa Baa, Black Sheep', we have already had occasion to notice; it is marred only very slightly by a certain amount of baby-talk at the beginning. The second, 'The Drums of the Fore and Aft', introduces us to children—or near-children—very different from Black Sheep and his sister. It introduces us, also, to the Indian Army, and it is a good place in which to see what at once fascinated and shocked Kipling's first readers.

'The Drums of the Fore and Aft' is the longest but one of the Indian stories, and we have an immediate sense that the writer is spreading himself. He gives a brief hint of his subject—the rout of an untried British infantry regiment during an Afghan campaign—and then turns to general reflections on army morale:

> The courage of the British soldier is officially supposed to be above proof, and, as a general rule, it is so. The exceptions are decently shovelled out of sight, only to be referred to in the freshest of unguarded talk that occasionally swamps a Mess-table at midnight. . . . The British soldier is not altogether to be blamed for occasional lapses; but this verdict he should not know. . . . He should be shot or hanged afterwards—to encourage the others; but he should not be vilified in newspapers, for that is want of tact and waste of time.

The unseasoned soldier, 'hampered by the intense selfishness of the lower classes, and unsupported by any regimental associations', will not be helped by modern plans for 'half-educating everything that wears trousers':

> Speaking roughly, you must employ either blackguards or gentlemen, or, best of all, blackguards commanded by gentlemen, to do butcher's work with efficiency and despatch. . . . Their officers are as good as good can be, because their training begins early, and God has arranged that a clean-run youth of the British middle classes shall, in the matter of backbone, brains, and bowels, surpass all other youths.

We have found here, within the space of a few paragraphs, a mingling of brutality and prejudice which is very disconcerting. Where does it come from? There is a poem in which

Kipling tells us that 'sometimes in a smoking-room, one learns why things were done'—and he is simply doing his best to catch the tone of smoking-room conversation as he must often have listened to it from the lips of impressively experienced, disllusioned and cynical Anglo-Indians. It must be partly from the same source, too, that there derives the intensely 'knowing' tone which pervades this and many other of his stories, and which, more than anything else, was to alienate professional critics. One comes to wonder whether even the Commander-in-Chief himself can know as much about the inner feelings, and right handling, of his Army as does young Mr. Kipling. But here there is an important point to be made. Kipling really did have a large first-hand acquaintance with the men he is dogmatizing about; indeed, we possess it on good authority that, before Kipling left India at the age of twenty-three, the Commander-in-Chief (Sir Frederick Roberts, later Lord Roberts of Kandahar) had actually consulted him on the state of feeling among the rank and file. This power was to remain with Kipling right up to his over-sheltered late middle age. His ceaseless curiosity was of a highly professional sort; like not a few other great writers, he tended to be interested in people simply for the knowledge of them, and of all their walks and ways, which he could squeeze or screw out of them. When, in his years of fame, he sailed regularly to and from South Africa every year, he is said to have been unpopular with the junior officers on the P. & O. liners. He would cultivate their acquaintance, suck them dry, and later complain to the directors of the shipping company that they were too ready to flirt with the women passengers.

But we must return to the regiment that was to be known as the Fore and Aft, and to the two drummer boys upon whom the story pivots. Jakin and Lew are 'a brace of the most finished little fiends that ever banged drum or tootled fife in the Band of a British Regiment'. Kipling does his best to bring their depravity graphically home to us, and he succeeds pretty well, in spite of certain reticences imposed upon him by the limits of what convention at that time judged it possible to print or refer to. The boys are about fourteen, and they drink, swear, and fight viciously between themselves and against others. But they are very tough; when they hear that the regiment is to go on active service they are determined not to miss a chance of glory; and they persuade their colonel to let them join that part of the Band that is to go to the front. 'The Colonel was well pleased,' we are told. 'If that was the temper of the children, what would not the men do?'

What the men in fact do is to break in the face of the enemy. The engagement in which this disgrace overtakes them is described in detail, and with quite astonishing authority. Here, at least, Kipling is working entirely at second-hand. India was a peaceful place during his seven years there, and (like Stephen Crane when he wrote *The Red Badge of Courage*) he had never been within sight or sound of a battlefield. Nor did he know the North-West Frontier, apart from a single glimpse obtained when, as a young newspaper man, he had travelled to Fort Jumrood at the mouth of the Khyber Pass to report the arrival of the Amir Abdurrahman on a state visit to the Viceroy. (On that occasion, indeed, he had contrived to take a stroll into the Pass itself, and turned back only when a tribesman took a pot shot at him.) So how did he come by the material for this tremendous and minutely realized battle-piece? From soldier's tales, we must suppose, for the most part. But there was something more. The last quarter of the nineteenth century was a kind of golden age of war correspondents and war artists. Every campaign or 'punitive expedition' was vividly reported in the English papers, and—since photography had not yet been applied in this sphere—even more vividly depicted in drawings and sketches supposed to have been executed on the spot. These highly dramatised pictures, in which screaming savages are seen spearing British soldiers, and British soldiers are shooting and bayoneting screaming savages in return, were familiar to every boy in England. Quite a lot of talent went into them, and they were permitted to be very gruesome indeed. Yet they all pale before Kipling's writing here, which powerfully evokes the whole psychology of battle.

The men of the Fore and Aft break and bolt, cursed and belaboured by their officers. Two tried regiments on either flank—one Highland, the other Gurkha—look on in horror and indignation. And then, between this routed force and the advancing but wary enemy Ghazis, Jakin and Lew appear, marching side by side, and summoning their comrades to retrieve their honour by making, on drum and fife, 'a hideous hash of the first bars of the "British Grenadiers" '.

> There was a far-off clapping of hands from the Gurkhas, and a roar from the Highlanders in the distance, but never a shot was fired by British or Afghan. The two little red dots moved forward in the open, parallel to the enemy's front.
>
> But of all the world's great heroes
> There's none that can compare,
> With a tow-row-row-row-row-row,
> To the British Grenadier!
>
> The men of the Fore and Aft were gathering thick at the entrance to the plain. The Brigadier on the heights far above was speechless with rage. Still no movement from the enemy. The day stayed to watch the children.

But it is not for long. As the Fore and Aft recover and reform, an Afghan volley drops both boys dead. And the story ends:

> But some say, and among these be the Gurkhas who watched on the hillside, that that battle was won by Jakin and Lew, whose little bodies were borne up just in time to fit two gaps at the head of the big ditch-grave for the dead under the heights of Jagai.

Yet this is not the whole story. When left by the rest of the Band (who could run faster), Jakin and Lew had found 'a cast-off water bottle, which naturally was full of canteen rum', and their heroic action was the consequence of drinking it. The popular literature of the nineteenth century has many drummer-boys and buglers who die a glorious death in heartening their fellows. We are not being told that Jakin and Lew do *not* do this; the manner of their death is simply part of our learning (as in a smoking-room) '*why* things were done'. And, as often in Kipling, what may at first seem very crude is in fact rather subtle.

There is a point here, indeed, that may be missed. Kipling poured out both poems and stories so profusely in the early years of his career as an author, and dealt so much in strong accents and broad effects, that we may be inclined to overlook the disciplined craftsmanship which marks nearly all his writing. Respect for faithful workmanship was something that came to him from his father and his father's circle; he retained it throughout his years as a journalist; and it was seldom to desert him thereafter. His earliest masterpiece, 'The Man who would be King' (*The Phantom Rickshaw*, 1888), written when he was twenty-two, leaves on a first reading simply the effect of a *tour de force* of the imagination, of a fantastic story rendered fantastically convincing. But a closer examination shows how much of its power is owing to the deliberate artistry with which it is constructed. Kipling is here employing what was always to be one of his most effective devices, that of the 'frame'. The story proper is, as it were, set back behind an outer narrative which in one way or another enhances its effect. Let us digress for a moment to look at the first paragraph of 'Love-o'-Women', a great story, but one to which we shall not recur:

> The horror, the confusion, and the separation of the murderer from his comrades were all over before I came. There remained only on the barrack-square the blood of man calling from the ground. The hot sun had dried it to a dusky gold-beater's-skin film, cracked lozenge-wise by the heat; and as the wind rose, each lozenge, rising a little, curled up at the edges as if it were a dumb tongue. Then a heavier gust blew all away down wind in grains of dark-coloured dust. It was too hot to stand in the sunshine before breakfast. The men were in barracks talking the matter over. A knot of soldiers' wives stood by one of the entrances to the married quarters, while inside a woman shrieked and raved with wicked filthy words.

This tremendous opening soon reveals itself as *outside* the story we are to be told; it renders concrete, in a single swift and violent action, the whole world of Indian barrack-room life in which the events of 'Love-o'-Women' are generated.

In 'The Man who would be King' the frame has both this function and another one as well. The narrator's world (which is Kipling's world when he was working for the *Civil and Military Gazette*) is an uncomfortable world, and odd things happen in it; it is accustomed to tidings from remote places ('the telephone-bell is ringing madly, and Kings are being killed on the Continent')—and it is aware, too, of things savage and horrible happening in Native States which are not remote at all. This narrator's world is itself exotic enough to prepare us a little for the almost incredibly strange world of the main story, while at the same time it enhances that strangeness by being itself, in essentials, secure and humdrum. It is at once bridge and chasm.

The story takes its start from an actual incident in Kipling's own life—which is perhaps sufficient warrant for calling the narrator 'Kipling' throughout. He is travelling on some normal newspaper assignment, and has run out of money, so his railway ticket is neither First-class nor Second-class but Intermediate, 'which is very awful indeed':

> There are no cushions in the Intermediate class, and the population are either Intermediate, which is Eurasian, or Native, which for a long night journey is nasty, or Loafer, which is amusing though intoxicated. Intermediates do not buy from refreshment-rooms. They carry their food in bundles and pots, and buy sweets from the native sweetmeat-sellers, and drink the roadside water. That is why in the hot weather Intermediates are taken out of the carriages dead, and in all weathers are most properly looked down upon.

Kipling falls into conversation with a Loafer, a low-class English adventurer, who appears to have been a private soldier at one time, and who is anxious to send a message to a friend who will be travelling on a train which Kipling could contact later on his own journey. In this context he speaks of one dishonest trick by which he gets a living: that of pretending to be a correspondent of Kipling's own paper, and so extorting money from petty native rulers and others by ferreting out their misdeeds and threatening them with exposure. At present he has been cherishing lively expectations on the score of what such a ruler, the Degumber Rajah, did to his father's widow:

> 'What did he do to his father's widow, then?'
>
> 'Filled her up with red pepper and slippered her to death as she hung from a beam. I found that out myself, and I'm the only man that would dare going into the State to get hush-money for it. They'll try to poison me, same as they did in Chortumna when I went on the loot there. But you'll give the man at Marwar Junction my message?'

Kipling promises to give the message. But he is experienced enough to know very well the kind of situation he is dealing with:

> I had heard, more than once, of men personating correspondents of newspapers and bleeding small Native States with threats of exposure, but I had never met any of the caste before. They lead a hard life, and generally die with great suddenness. The Native States have a wholesome horror of English newspapers which may throw light on their peculiar methods of government. . . . They are the dark places of the earth, full of unimaginable cruelty, touching the Railway and the Telegraph on one side, and, on the other, the days of Harun-al-Raschid.

Kipling delivers the message (it is no more than 'He has gone South for the week'), the recipient being a big man with a red beard. Later he reflects that he had better put a stop to the particular mischief these scoundrels are brewing, and he takes steps which result in their being prevented from entering Degumber. We are now some way into the 'frame' of the story, and we have had a glimpse of the kind of thing that happens in 'the dark places of the earth'. Kipling returns to the routine of his newspaper office, and for two or three pages the story appears to come to a halt in favour of a vivid account of the discomforts of the place during the hot season:

> One Saturday night it was my pleasant duty to put the paper to bed alone. A King or a courtier or courtesan of a Community was going to die or get a new Constitution, or do something that was important on the other side of the world, and the paper was to be held open till the latest possible minute in order to catch the telegram.
>
> It was a pitchy black night, as stifling as a June night can be, and the *loo*, the red-hot wind from the westward, was booming among the tinder-dry trees and pretending that the rain was on its heels. Now and again a spot of almost boiling water would fall on the dust with the flop of a frog, but all our weary world knew that was only pretence. It was a shade cooler in the press-room than the office, so I sat there, while the type ticked and clicked, and the night-jars hooted at the windows, and the all but naked compositors wiped the

> sweat from their foreheads, and called for water. . . . There was no special reason beyond the heat and worry to make tension, but, as the clock-hands crept up to three o'clock, and the machines spun their fly-wheels two or three times to see that all was in order before I said the word that would set them off, I could have shrieked aloud.

And then, suddenly, the two adventurers appear, looking for 'him as turned us back from the Degumer State'. But their object is not to make trouble; they are merely seeking information about Kafiristan, an almost unknown territory to the north-west of Afghanistan. India, they feel, has ceased to give them adequate scope. They are going to Kafiristan, and are resolved to be kings there.

The two men enlarge on their crazy proposal. The red-bearded Daniel Dravot is the dominant partner; Peachey Carnehan, Kipling's former fellow traveller, takes second place. Dravot asks for drink, saying, 'The Contrack doesn't begin yet'; he remarks that the women of Kafiristan are very beautiful. 'But that is provided against in the Contrack,' Carnehan says, 'Neither Women nor Liqu-or, Daniel.' We have a good idea of what is meant by the 'Contrack', and we suspect that Dravot is less likely to stick to it than Carnehan. But it is Dravot who puts their plan succinctly:

> 'And that's all we know, except that no one has gone there, and they fight; and in any place where they fight, a man who knows how to drill men can always be a King. We shall go to those parts and say to any King we find—"D'you want to vanquish your foes?" and we will show him how to drill men; for that we know better than anything else. Then we will subvert that King and seize his Throne and establish a Dy-nasty.'

Kipling scarcely takes the strange couple seriously, although, as he leaves them for the night, they are still poring intently over his books and maps. They tell him to be sure to come to the Serai—a great market-square—next morning. He does so, and discovers that they are not only in earnest but also formidably resourceful and intelligent. Dravot has disguised himself as a mad priest, and Carnehan as his servant. They are loading two camels with crude toys, which they declare they are taking to Kabul, the capital of Afghanistan, to sell to the Amir himself. As Kipling sees them depart in quest of their kingdom he reflects that they may just manage to wander through Afghanistan without detection, but that, beyond, they will find death—certain and awful death. Ten days later, he happens to hear that a mad priest has passed through Peshawur, and joined a caravan bound for Kabul. And he records: 'The two, then, were beyond the Border. I would have prayed for them, but, that night, a real King died in Europe, and demanded an obituary notice.' The rest of the story tells us how Daniel Dravot himself became a real king, after all, and Peachey Carnehan a king along with him. We may think of it, too, as *their* obituary. They are fortunate in having Rudyard Kipling to write it. For it is savage but splendid.

Three years pass; there is another hot night in the office, another strained waiting for something to be telegraphed from the other side of the world, 'exactly as had happened before'. And suddenly somebody is standing beside Kipling. Or not quite standing—for it is only 'what was left of a man', bent into a circle, wrapped in rags, and unable to move except by bringing his feet one over the other like a bear. Peachey Carnehan has come back. He recounts his history, painfully but vividly. Sometimes he lapses into mere incoherence, for his mind is as broken as his body and he has no clear sense of his own identity. Was it Dravot who was prodded to his death on the rope bridge, or was it Carnehan? He is not quite sure. But the mental darkness which thus from time to time obscures the story merely serves to throw the total picture into brilliant relief.

Only the great masters of fiction can give to their creations so much of the very breath of life as Kipling here achieves—testing for the first time the real reach of his art. It is partly a matter of the particularity with which first, every step of the men's journey, and next, every move towards their conquest of power, are explored and reported to us. It is rather more a matter of deep penetration into the springs of action. One of Kipling's few close friends in later life was to be, as we shall see, Rider Haggard, the author of *She* and *King Solomon's Mines*, compelling romances of wild adventure in dark places. And this is the superficial face of 'The Man who would be King'. Yet Kipling's story belongs to quite a different world of the imagination. It is a world in which Daniel Dravot's dream of empire is one with Alexander's (he founds much hope on the fact that his subjects are so light of skin, and Alexander's actual armies may have set this stamp upon them)—and one, also, with that greater *raj* in which Kipling so fervently believed, and of which in his finest poem, 'Recessional', he was so majestically to sing the dirge, without quite knowing what he did. *The captains and the kings depart* . . . They depart, very horribly, in 'The Man who would be King'.

They depart because Dravot, faced by an inactive winter season, breaks the 'Contrack' and demands a wife. His sway over his scattered kingdom has been beneficent; he is a blackguard who understands as well as any Viceroy of India the purposes of the *pax Britannica*. He knows what he has achieved, and could say with Virgil—although he has never heard of him—*Tantae molis erat Romanam condere gentem*. He is a big man—but finally not quite big enough: not, when it comes to the crunch, as big as Carnehan, his lieutenant. When the splendour of his conception gets too big for him he cracks—and produces reasons why he should have a wife. It seems an unimportant decision; to his people he is as a god; and, in fact, a wife is produced. But when he kisses her publicly she bites him, drawing blood—and instantly his subjects are subjects no longer. Kipling's supreme power is an intuitive understanding of some of the most primitive layers of consciousness, and here we do not doubt for a moment the reality of the *tabu* that has been violated. Dravot is blind to the last and heroic to the last: 'Cut, you beggars,' he shouts, after he has shaken hands with Carnehan and walked to the middle of the bridge. Carnehan, implicated in a disaster he had done nothing to bring about, meets a harder fate. He is crucified between two pine-trees, and is still alive and screaming next day. As this is regarded as a miracle, he is taken down and his life preserved. 'They was cruel enough to feed him up in the temple,' he says, speaking hazily of himself in the third person, 'because they said he was more of a God than old Daniel that was a man'. He crawls back to India, and eventually into Kipling's office. He tells his story. And then:

> He fumbled in the mass of rags round his bent waist; brought out a black horsehair bag embroidered with silver thread,

> and shook therefrom on to my table—the dried, withered head of Daniel Dravot! The morning sun that had long been paling the lamps struck the red beard and blind sunken eyes; struck, too, a heavy circlet of gold studded with raw turquoises, that Carnehan placed tenderly on the battered temples.
>
> 'You behold now,' said Carnehan, 'the Emperor in his habit as he lived—the King of Kafiristan with his crown upon his head. Poor old Daniel that was a monarch once!'

As well as having the function of authenticating Carnehan's incredible tale, the withered head and its crown afford a bravura close to the tale. Within a day or two, we are finally told, Carnehan is dead.

Anybody who has read 'The Man who would be King' is likely to have his attention arrested by the title of another of Kipling's Indian stories, 'The Man who Was' (*Life's Handicap*, 1891). This is to some extent a companion piece, for it too has as its subject the reappearance in India of the ruins of what had been a man. Only this man is an officer and a gentleman, and the story is set in the mess of a crack British regiment, Her Majesty's White Hussars, quartered in the city of Peshawur. There is a formal dinner in honour of a visiting polo team from another regiment. Outside, Pathan marauders may be creeping about in the dark in an attempt to steal British rifles, but within the mess the ritual of such a dinner goes on undisturbed. It is rather a splendid affair, and it has its culminating moment:

> The talk rose higher and higher, and the regimental band played between the courses, as is the immemorial custom, till all tongues ceased for a moment with the removal of the dinner-slips and the first toast of obligation when an officer rising said, 'Mr. Vice, the Queen,' and little Mildred from the bottom of the table answered, 'The Queen, God bless her,' and the big spurs clanked as the big men heaved themselves up and drank the Queen upon whose pay they were falsely supposed to settle their mess-bills. That Sacrament of the Mess never grows old, and never ceases to bring a lump into the throat of the listener wherever he be by sea or land.

We may not like 'Sacrament of the Mess', but we shall notice the skill with which the little joke about mess-bills (an officer needed a private income to be in a regiment like the White Hussars) is made to act, for the moment, as a slightly deflationary device, holding down our own emotional response (if we have one) to the toast. There is a reason for this. Kipling is saving up for the crisis of the story.

In addition to the visiting team there is another guest: a Russian Cossack officer, Dirkovitch, whom the mysterious ways of the Government of India have imposed upon the White Hussars for a time. Dirkovitch is a most unpleasant and unmannerly person. But this is an aristocratic mess, and its courtesy towards him remains impeccable. The true guest of honour is a native officer, Rissaldar Hira Singh, 'the cadet of a royal house, the son of a king's son'. He has played a brilliant game for the visitors, and when he joins the mess for dessert (his religion would have made it impossible for him to dine with his British brother-officers) his health is drunk with enthusiasm. He makes an appropriate reply, ending on a martial note which he might not have touched had not his eye fallen upon Dirkovitch lolling back in his chair:

> 'But if by the will of God there arises any other game which is not the polo game, then be assured, Colonel Sahib and officers, that we will play it out side by side, though *they*,' again his eye sought Dirkovitch, 'though *they*, I say, have fifty ponies to our one horse.' And with a deep-mouthed *Rung-ho!* that sounded like a musket-butt on flagstones, he sat down amid leaping glasses.

We have to remember here that, at the end of the nineteenth century, every British soldier in India believed that it was his destiny, at some early date, to confront and repel the invading armies of imperial Russia.

Suddenly there is the sound of a shot outside, and then a scuffle and a cry of pain. At this point the story takes on tremendous impetus:

> 'Carbine-stealing again!' said the Adjutant, calmly sinking back in his chair. 'This comes of reducing the guards. I hope the sentries have killed him.'

The feet of armed men pounded on the verandah flags, and it was as though something was being dragged.

'Why don't they put him in the cells till the morning?' said the Colonel testily. 'See if they've damaged him, sergeant.'

The mess sergeant fled out into the darkness and returned with two troopers and a corporal, all very much perplexed.

'Caught a man stealin' carbines, sir,' said the corporal. 'Leastways 'e was crawlin' towards the barricks, sir, past the main road sentries, an' the sentry 'e sez, sir——'

The limp heap of rags upheld by the three men groaned. Never was seen so destitute and demoralised an Afghan. He was turbanless, shoeless, caked with dirt, and all but dead with rough handling. Hira Singh started slightly at the sound of the man's pain. Dirkovitch took another glass of brandy.

'*What* does the sentry say?' said the Colonel.

'Sez 'e speaks English, sir,' said the corporal.

'So you brought him into mess instead of handing him over to the sergeant! If he spoke all the Tongues of the Pentecost you've no business——'

Again the bundle groaned and muttered. Little Mildred had risen from his place to inspect. He jumped back as though he had been shot.

'Perhaps it would be better, sir, to send the men away,' said he to the Colonel, for he was a much privileged subaltern. He put his arms round the rag-bound horror as he spoke, and dropped him into a chair.

'Little' Mildred (he is six feet four and big in proportion) has seen a gleam of the truth. But meanwhile the mess stare in horror at this broken creature, who weeps like a child and who cringes in inexplicable fear when Dirkovitch addresses him in Russian. Then it gradually becomes apparent that the captured man is on ground dimly familiar to him. He puts out a hand and touches the hidden mechanism that ingeniously transforms the shape of a seven-branched candlestick—one of the mess's most elaborate pieces of silver plate. He speaks incoherently of a missing horse—and some realise that he refers to a painting removed from the mess-room in 1867. Then he tumbles into a chair: Mildred's chair, as it happens, at the bottom of the table. At this, Mildred has an inspiration:

> Little Mildred stood at the Colonel's side talking in his ear. 'Will you be good enough to take your seats, please, gentlemen!' he said, and the mess dropped into the chairs. . . . The wide-eyed mess-sergeant filled the glasses in dead silence. Once more the Colonel rose, but his hand shook, and the port spilled on the table as he looked straight at the man in little Mildred's chair and said hoarsely, 'Mr. Vice, the Queen.' There was a little pause, but the man sprang to his feet and answered without hesitation, 'The Queen, God bless her!' and as he emptied the thin glass he snapped the shank between his fingers.

The mess has long ago dropped the expensive custom of instantly snapping the stem of any glass from which the Queen's health had been drunk. But everybody knows about it. So here is a moment of complete revelation—and a moment scarcely anywhere surpassed by Kipling in point of sheer theatrical effect. The returned officer of the White Hussars is quickly identified, and Dirkovitch meanwhile has got the essence of his story out of him in Russian, and unblushingly communicates it to his hosts. During the Crimean War Lieutenant Austin Limmason had been captured by the Russians before Sebastopol, and through some act of private malice had been treated not as a prisoner of war but as a convict. After thirty years in Siberia, and bearing on his body the scars of savage punishment, he has escaped and made his way (mysteriously, we may feel) back to his old regiment. And very soon he is dead:

> The Lieutenant had returned only to go away again three days later, when the wail of the Dead March, and the tramp of the squadrons, told the wondering Station, who saw no gap in the mess-table, that an officer of the regiment had resigned his new-found commission.

In this impressive story, as in many others, Kipling is elaborating and dramatizing an existent army legend. But he is doing something else as well. The story begins thus:

> Let it be clearly understood that the Russian is a delightful person till he tucks in his shirt. As an Oriental he is charming. It is only when he insists upon being treated as the most

easterly of western peoples instead of the most westerly of easterns that he becomes a racial anomaly extremely difficult to handle.

It ends with Dirkovitch being 'handled' with unflinching courtesy still. When at length he takes his leave of the White Hussars, Mildred and another officer see him to his train:

'Good-bye Dirkovitch, and a pleasant journey,' said little Mildred.

'*Au revoir*,' said the Russian.

'Indeed! But we thought you were going home?'

'Yes, but I will come again. My dear friends, is that road shut?' He pointed to where the North Star burned over the Khyber Pass.

'By Jove! I forgot. Of course. Happy to meet you, old man, any time you like. Got everything you want? Cheroots, ice, bedding? That's all right. Well, *au revoir*, Dirkovitch.'

'Um,' said the other man, as the tail-lights of the train grew small. 'Of—all—the—unmitigated——!'

Little Mildred answered nothing, but watched the North Star and hummed a selection from a recent Simla burlesque that had much delighted the White Hussars. It ran—

I'm sorry for Mister Bluebeard,
I'm sorry to cause him pain;
But a terrible spree there's sure to be
When he comes back again.

The lines 'which had much delighted the White Hussars' may remind us of certain more famous lines, first heard in a London Music Hall in 1878:

We don't want to fight, but, by
jingo if we do,
We've got the ships, we've got the
men, we've got the money too.
We've fought the Bear before, and
while Britons shall be true,
The Russians shall not have Constantinople.

The song gave the word 'Jingoism' to the English language. There was already a literary word for it: 'Chauvinism', which the *Oxford Dictionary* defines as 'exaggerated and bellicose patriotism'. Some readers feel that Kipling has deployed great skill in writing just this pervasively into 'The Man who Was', and that what is acceptable in a Music Hall song is inapposite in a work of serious literary art. On the other hand, it may be maintained that the story reflects political realities—and political realities of rather a permanent sort.

If Kipling was very much a patriot, he was a patriot like John Milton, who knew that 'Peace hath her victories no less renowned than war'. Many of the stories are about Anglo-Indian civilians, and some of them set out to make very clear that the Indian Civil Service had a right to its name. It is true that, in the political sphere, his constant attitude to the indigenous inhabitants of India exemplified what we now call 'paternalism', and that he was often to express convictions that it is unfashionable to utter publicly today. In the volume *In Black and White* (1888) there is a vivid description of a communal riot during the Mohammedan festival of Mohurram; it is suppressed by British troops who have not too much regard for 'the toes of Hindu and Mussulman'; and finally Kipling draws the moral:

> If an advance be made all credit is given to the native, while the Englishmen stand back and wipe their foreheads. If a failure occurs, the Englishmen step forward and take the blame. Overmuch tenderness of this kind has bred a strong belief among many natives that the native is capable of administering the country, and many devout Englishmen believe this also, because the theory is stated in beautiful English with all the latest political colours.

This sounds like the mutterings of a disgruntled old *sahib* in a club. But again we must notice how much political reality is mixed up with it. Great Britain had taken over an India so chaotic as to be rather like a communal riot on a colossal scale, and was in fact to build so well there that one day, when the 'natives' *were* capable of administering the country, they astonished the world by effectively preserving the institutions of parliamentary democracy. Most of Kipling's English administrators, indeed, are not concerned with such long perspectives; flood and plague and drought and famine are immediately around them, and they cope as they can. Afterwards they may retreat, swearing, to their clubs, but they have done a man-sized job, all the same. Kipling's most effective celebration of this fully historical aspect of the *raj* is in a story called 'William the Conqueror' (*The Day's Work*, 1898).

William Martyn is a girl, and we never learn her true Christian name. She has come out from England at the age of nineteen in order to keep house for her brother, who is an Acting District Superintendent of Police. We are made to realize at once that such people are far from living in any kind of luxury. To save the expense of going even to a cheap hill station, William has 'stayed down three hot weathers' in her bleak little four-roomed bungalow:

> There were the usual blue-and-white striped jail-made rugs on the uneven floor; the usual glass-studded Amritsar *phulkaris* draped to nails driven into the flaking whitewash of the walls; the usual half-dozen chairs that did not match, picked up at sales of dead men's effects. . . . It was as though everything had been unpacked the night before to be repacked next morning. Not a door in the house was true on its hinges. The little windows, fifteen feet up, were darkened with wasp-nests, and lizards hunted flies between the beams of the wood-ceiled roof. . . . Thus did people live who had such an income.

For four years William has enjoyed herself hugely, although—or because—her life has been hazardous as well as comfortless. She has been through a very bad cholera year, 'seeing sights unfit to be told'; has herself had six weeks of typhoid fever—during which her head was shaved, so that she now wears her hair cropped and curling; has twice been nearly drowned while fording a river on horseback; and can speak Urdu and even rough Punjabi fluently. She rides to dances with a shawl thrown over her skirt, acts in amateur theatricals, plays the banjo, rules 'eight servants and two horses, their accounts and their diseases', and can look men slowly and deliberately between the eyes, even after they have proposed to her and been rejected. She has not much use for irrelevant things, like writing home to her aunts and reading the English magazines, or for irrelevant people:

> 'I like men who do things,' she had confided to a man in the Educational Department, who was teaching the sons of cloth merchants and dyers the beauty of Wordsworth's 'Excursion' in annotated cram-books; and when he grew poetical, William explained that she 'didn't understand poetry very much; it made her head ache', and another broken heart took refuge at the Club. But it was all William's fault. She delighted in hearing men talk of their own work, and that is the most fatal way of bringing a man to your feet.

In particular she likes to hear her brother talking shop with his friend Scott, an impecunious irrigation engineer: of 'canals and the policing of canals . . . of the transplanting bodily of villages to newly irrigated ground, and of the coming fight with the desert in the south'.

Suddenly, far in the south, an even more urgent fight is on. A vast region has been hit by famine and disease, and from all over India every Englishman with the right reputation is mustered for a fearful struggle. Both Scott and Martyn receive the summons. William, who has heard that the senior official directing the operation has his wife with him, manages to get taken along too. 'She's as clever as a man, confound her,' her brother tells Scott in explanation. 'A famine's no place for a woman,' Scott replies. We realize that for Scott William *is* a woman—despite the nickname which signals her having been admitted on a man's terms to a man's world.

Scott and William are in love—but not a word is spoken, or a glance exchanged, for so long as the famine is 'sore on the land'. There is a moment of supreme test when Scott, passing within a few miles of the place where William is in camp, does not turn aside to visit her. 'It wouldn't be him if he did,' she says. Scott is resourceful as well as devoted. Having been largely provided with kinds of grain so unfamiliar to the starving people that they refuse to eat it, he feeds it to an ever increasing herd of goats, and thus gains milk with which to save the lives of children. The plan obliges him to give up riding and to 'pace slowly at the head of his flocks . . . as more babies and more goats were added to him'. He feels this shepherd's role to be an absurdity, and knows that it will be held as a joke against him for the rest of his days. But, when he comes in this strange guise to William's camp, the story, for a beautiful moment, turns from epic to pastoral:

> He had no desire to make any dramatic entry, but an accident of the sunset ordered it that, when he had taken off his helmet to get the evening breeze, the low light should fall across his forehead, and he could not see what was before him; while one waiting at the tent door beheld, with new eyes, a young man, beautiful as Paris, a god in a halo of golden dust, walking slowly at the head of his flocks, while at his knee ran small naked Cupids.

William (who 'doesn't understand poetry very much') is enormously amused. She is still doing her own untiring part of the day's work. Like Scott and everybody else concerned in the rescue operation, she has driven herself to the last limit of her physical endurance.

At length the famine is conquered. Scott and William, now engaged to be married, travel north in the same train, and others join them:

> They were picking them up at almost every station now—men and women coming in for the Christmas Week, with racquets, with bundles of polo-sticks, with dear and bruised cricket-bats, with fox-terriers and saddles. . . . Scott was with the bachelors at the far end of the train, where they chaffed him mercilessly about feeding babies and milking goats; but from time to time he would stroll up to William's window, and murmur: 'Good enough, isn't it?' and William would answer with sighs of pure delight: 'Good enough, indeed.' The large open names of the home towns were good to listen to. Umballa, Ludianah, Phillour, Jullundur, they rang like the coming marriage-bells in her ears.

The story ends with Christmas carols:

> Mark my footsteps well, my page.
> Tread thou in them boldly

—and:

> When shepherds watched their flocks
> by night. . . .

'William the Conqueror' concludes on this note—and with tears in William's eyes. Such a close is appropriate enough in a story which itself makes rather a vigorous assault on our emotions. It is not difficult to make fun of the whole thing. 'I knew he was *pukka*,' Scott's chief says admiringly, 'but I didn't know he was as *pukka* as this!' The tone would be right in a story written for the edification of Boy Scouts and Girl Guides, and we may feel that this particular vision of British India has been constructed a little too much with an eye to our admiration. Yet no story expresses more clearly just what Kipling conceived 'the white man's burden' to be—or, indeed, his perception that accepting it is to accept at the same time certain inevitable limitations in personal relationships and individual development.

CHAPTER FIVE

THE CONQUEST OF LONDON AND *THE LIGHT THAT FAILED*

IT IS IMPOSSIBLE to read the Indian stories without realizing that their author was a man who found almost everything and everybody in the subcontinent absorbingly interesting. Nevertheless there are signs that, towards the end of his 'seven years' hard', Kipling was chafing to get away. He had made a name for himself while absurdly young—but it was as an author, which was not a class of person particularly attended to in Anglo-Indian society. (William and her friends, we must suppose, would have judged the Indian Railway Library to be full of rattling good yarns, but would scarcely have ranked their inventor among 'men who do things'.) It was in England that he must win his way, and at five thousand miles remove this was no easy thing to plan for. That he could be at sea about English taste is amusingly evident in the history of his first attempt to get a story into an English magazine.

He appears to have felt that something really sensational was required, and that he had better turn out a tale which would have made Edgar Allan Poe himself shudder. This he did in a story of which a later, and apparently chastened, version is to be found in *Life's Handicap*. Its title there is 'The Mark of the Beast'. It tells how a drunken Englishman desecrates a temple, and is embraced by a leper who, in addition to *being* a leper, is unfortunately possessed of some sort of supernatural power. The Englishman then rapidly develops all the characteristics of a wolf, and it is only when the leper is captured and persuaded by some hours of frightful torture to be of a better mind that the spell is lifted and the possessed man recovers. This story—or rather the more gruesome early version—was sent to London and came into the hands of Andrew Lang, an important literary figure who, among other things, was a charming writer for children. Lang declared that he would have given five pounds never to have seen 'this poisonous stuff', and then passed the story on to William Sharp, an author of mild romantic verse who was later, as 'Fiona Macleod', to publish equally mild romantic prose. Sharp made two guesses about the writer of this shocking tale: that he was very young, and that he would die mad before reaching the age of thirty. Kipling died at the age of seventy, and if he was ever mad he was wise enough to keep quiet about it.

Another reason for wanting to get away from India may have been a sense of something anomalous in his social position; on grand occasions he was uncertain whether he was present as the celebrated son of distinguished parents or as somebody sent along to write up the event for a newspaper. This made his manners, which had never taken on much polish, additionally uncertain, and he could be assertive or aggressive on unsuitable occasions. But another problem must have been more important than this. The Family Square was still solid, although Trix was soon to announce her engagement to John Fleming, a soldier working in the Survey Department, and so eminently a man who 'did things'. Lockwood Kipling was still as multifariously interested as ever; on Ruddy's last visit to Lahore he insisted on their going out together and learning to fly kites after the fashion of Punjabi children. But his parents lived what Kipling judged to be an extremely quiet life, all the same; and we may suspect that they were not in a hurry to provide their admired son with attractive female society. It was an age in which social convention made it peculiarly difficult at least for diffident young men (and in this sphere Kipling was diffident) to get to know girls at all well; and this is the reason why so many of them passed through a phase of blameless attachment to some older—and generally married—woman. Kipling got away from too much emotional dependence on the Square in just this way. The lady, Mrs. Hill, was an American from Beaver, Pennsylvania, who was married to a solid and unspectacular professor of science in Allahabad. She was aged about thirty, clever and lively, and she took to Kipling at once. But there is no reason to suppose that her feeling for him was in the least romantic, or other than congruous with what she reported of her first meeting with him:

> When we were seated at table and conversation was in full swing, my partner called my attention to a short dark-haired man of uncertain age, with a heavy moustache and wearing very thick glasses. . . . Mr. Kipling looks about forty, as he is

> beginning to go bald, but he is in reality just twenty-two. He was animation itself, telling his stories admirably, so that those about him were kept in gales of laughter. . . . He is certainly worth knowing, and we shall ask him to dinner soon.

Kipling was quickly the intimate friend of the Hills, spending much time under their roof; and when he was away from them he wrote to Mrs. Hill almost every day. When she decided, after a serious illness, to avoid a 'hot weather' in India by making a trip along with her husband to visit her relations in Pennsylvania, returning to India by way of England, Kipling decided to join them as a travelling companion. He had saved a little money, and could make more by sending back travel-sketches for the *Pioneer*. The party left Calcutta in March 1889, travelling at a leisurely pace by Rangoon, Singapore and Hong Kong, and then spending a month in Japan before sailing for San Francisco. Kipling tarried four months in the United States, and contrived to get about a good deal. He would not thus have deferred going on to London had he not been fascinated by North America. Unfortunately he was already a celebrity in a small way; much of what it occurred to him to say got printed in newspapers; and much of this in its turn was in one way or another outrageous. His first recorded remark was perhaps the most startling of the lot:

> When the *City of Peking* steamed through the Golden Gate I saw with great joy that the blockhouse which guarded the mouth of the 'finest harbour in the world, sir', could be silenced by two gunboats from Hong Kong with safety, comfort and despatch.

What is striking about Kipling's unfavourable comments upon the American scene is the speed with which he delivered himself of them. We almost have the impression of being once more in the presence of the small boy who shouted: 'There's an angry Ruddy coming!' In the man as in the boy there was undoubtedly a native aggressiveness and belligerency, and this very readily declared itself in an unreasoned xenophobia.

Were this the whole story of Kipling's reaction to America—impatient dislike and a disposition to shout it around—there would be very little to interest us in it. In point of fact, however, he was deeply and powerfully attracted to America and American ways of life; and he thus becomes almost the classical instance of the ambivalence of feeling—the love-hate relationship, as it may be called—which has so frequently been at play across the Atlantic. His case instances, too, the particular trickiness attending the development of divergent national cultures within the framework of a common language. Had Kipling's native tongue been German or French, Urdu or Punjabi, his bad-tempered and bad-mannered chatter could have gained no instant currency in the country in which he had presented himself as a guest; and thrusting newspaper reporters, eager for copy, would not have caught him out to the same extent before better knowledge had prompted him to more moderate views. Yet, as time moves on, he is seen not so much to moderate his opinions as to form an alternative set of discrepant ones. And some of his enthusiasms were as superficially grounded as his dislikes; being very susceptible to the myths of Race and Blood, he indulged the notion that, when Empire and Republic are set side by side, the resulting spectacle is that of Anglo-Saxons (who are the whitest of all white men) gloriously spanning the globe. Anglo-American accord, at whatever level, is something a good deal more complicated than that.

Kipling, being himself a thrusting newspaper reporter, made sure of meeting anybody whose acquaintance he was resolved to secure. Chief among these was Mark Twain. He ran him to earth at Elmira, New York, in his brother-in-law's house, shook his hand, smoked two of his cigars, was favoured with a great deal of conversation, and departed mysteriously qualified to reproduce this *verbatim* as a long 'interview' printed in newspapers throughout America. The record of this occasion is now to be found in *From Sea to Sea* (1899), along with other of the travel sketches sent to the *Pioneer* from the United States. It is a fair example of the lively and vivid, if often slightly vulgar, reporting that Kipling turned out abundantly at this time.

Still in the company of the Hills, he sailed from New York in the autumn of 1889, reaching Liverpool on 5th October. The future held in store for him a much more intimate relationship with the United States.

In English literary history 1890 is very much Kipling's year.

No writer since Lord Byron had enjoyed so sudden a rise to fame. To some extent a way had been prepared for him; editors and publishers were aware of the youth who had been gaining a precocious celebrity in India; there were writers and critics (among them Andrew Lang, unconscious that here was the author of that revolting short story) who prepared to welcome him, elect him to their particular preserve, the Savile Club, and give him a great deal of advice—some of it valuable, and some of it confusing and contradictory. But with all this he would have been no more than a short season's wonder but for the leap to maturity which his writing achieved in this astonishingly prolific year. Marvellously although he had already written of India (most marvellously of all, some would maintain, in 'The Man who would be King'), he produced his strongest succession of Indian stories now: 'The Courting of Dinah Shadd', 'The Man who Was', 'Without Benefit of Clergy', 'On Greenhow Hill' (all in *Life's Handicap*). Simultaneously with this, he took an equally astonishing leap in verse. In India he had already published *Departmental Ditties* (1886), witty and topical pieces, soaked in the colour and personalities of the official world around him. In London he began to write the poems soon to be collected as *Barrack Room Ballads* (1892), which was to be for a generation the most popular and widely-selling of all volumes of English verse.

As a consequence of all this there was a Kipling boom in England which, within a few years, was to bring him wealth. There was an even greater Kipling boom in America which, but for the unsatisfactory state of copyright agreements, would have brought him much more. But in this first London year he was not well off. He took rooms, 'small, not over-clean or well-kept', in a building off the Strand and overlooking the Thames Embankment—a district, he says, 'primitive and passionate in its habits and population'. But in one particular Villiers Street was satisfactory. Sitting at his desk, he could look out of his window 'through the fan-light of Gatti's Music-Hall entrance, across the street, almost on to the stage'. He took to frequenting Gatti's himself; the fourpence which was the price of admission beguilingly included 'a pewter of beer or porter'. And it was from Gatti's as a place of popular entertainment that he got the idea for his new kind of poetry:

> The smoke, the roar, and the good-fellowship of relaxed humanity at Gatti's 'set' the scheme for a certain kind of song. The Private Soldier in India I thought I knew fairly well. His English brother (in the Guards mostly) sat and sang at my elbow any night I chose. . . . The outcome was the first of some verses called *Barrack-Room Ballads*.

This, as we shall see later, is not the whole truth about the origins of Kipling's most characteristic verse, but it is a large part of it. He cannot be said to have written for the common people in any substantial sense; but he had a much better understanding of them than had most of his contemporaries, and to this he joined a far greater interest in the multifarious workaday world around him than was exhibited by any other eminent English writer of the age. This is why, when he became unfashionable with people professionally concerned with literature, or with a public having taste and opportunity to cultivate its enjoyment, he remained the favourite writer of a far wider public—a public consisting, in the main, of men (and women) 'who do things'.

If he liked Gatti's, it was perhaps because it took him away from that literary society which he had come to London to conquer. We can see him doing his best to get on good terms with it, and on the whole it was disposed to be on good terms with him. The people who actively took him up and furthered his career were lightweights in the main, and his relations with the major writers of the age seem always to have been rather uncertain. Henry James was immensely struck by his talent, and indeed acknowledged his genius; he watched his development keenly, but to some final effect of disappointment. George Meredith, whom many regarded as the greatest of living English novelists and perhaps the greatest of living English poets as well, Kipling appears to have disliked at sight; he was 'an old withered little man' devoted to 'elaborated epigrammatic speech which on the first fizz strikes one as deuced good'. Thomas Hardy, a novelist of the first rank and soon to reveal himself, in late middle-age, as a poet of the first rank too, was to maintain courteous and friendly relations with him. With his own contemporaries and elder contemporaries, many of them belonging very consciously to what has come to be called 'the aesthetic movement', he was never at ease. Not many weeks after establishing himself in

London he sent back to the *Civil and Military* a set of resentful verses, in which he lamented having to consort with 'long-haired things' who 'moo and coo with womenfolk about their blessed souls'. Kipling longed for other company:

> It's Oh to meet an Army man,
> Set up, and trimmed and taut,
> Who does not spout hashed libraries
> Or think the next man's thought,
> And walks as though he owned himself,
> And hogs his bristles short.

His eventual move into isolation is often represented as due to his growing attachment to 'imperialist' and reactionary political views uncongenial both to middle-of-the-road conservative politicians and to liberal intellectuals and men of letters. But the seeds of this development were sown in these early London days, when he was at once brilliantly successful and—it is clear—maladjusted to, and terribly lonely in, his new environment. It was an environment the strangeness of which struck him at every level of his observation. He was, for example (to take a tiny instance), an Anglo-Indian who found it disturbing to go out to dinner where 'white women stood and waited on one behind one's chair'. And he was outraged by the manifest hypocrisy of people who derided his 'poor little Gods of the East' and asserted that the British in India spent violent lives '"oppressing" the Native', when they themselves let maid-servants of sixteen, 'at twelve or fourteen pounds per annum', haul 'thirty and forty pounds weight of bath-water at a time up four flights of stairs'.

In much of this feeling time has vindicated Kipling, and shown him as a man of deeper compassion, and thus more truly 'liberal', than many of the loud proclaimers of 'enlightened' views. Yet he might not have been so vehemently in revolt against the London scene had he not been at grips with some deep personal unhappiness at this time. This shows itself in all sorts of ways. He developed the sort of vindictive dislike of publishers and editors which more commonly characterizes wholly unsuccessful authors. In New York he had experienced some unfortunate passage of arms with the highly respectable firm of Harper Brothers, who are said to have dismissed him with the sombre words: 'Young man, this house is devoted to the production of literature.' In England he was soon convinced that he was up against an unscrupulous lot. Most young authors have to make the shocked discovery that publishers must stay in business. Kipling, who was intemperate in face of this situation, might have fallen into real difficulty but for the fact that he soon handed over this aspect of his affairs to A. P. Watt, a pioneer in the curious profession of 'literary agent', who thereafter sorted out his problems both in England (which was comparatively easy) and in the United States (which was very much more difficult).

But the root cause of his unhappiness at this time lay in some urgent sense of emotional insecurity. He had left the Family Square—and it had to be remembered that his parents were vital to him not merely as a troubled young man but as a writer as well. 'I think I can with truth say'—he was to record—'that those two made for me the only public for whom then I had any regard whatever till their deaths, in my forty-fifth year.' Mrs. Hill had returned to India, and although Kipling appears to have embarked upon a courtship of her younger sister, this had so little substance that it faded out on the score of his insufficient adherence to the Methodism into which he could be regarded as having been born. Much more shattering was a renewed contact, coming about through an accidental encounter in the street, with Flo Garrard. He discovered himself to be still in love with her, but could make no progress in her affections. Trix was to recall her as cold by nature, and as wanting 'to live her own life and paint her own very ineffective little pictures'. This estimate of Flo's talent we have to take on trust, since no specimens of her painting are known to have survived. Ironically enough, her only memorial is to be found in the most ambitious single work of the lover she had rejected.

Almost from the start of Kipling's career as a creative writer, it would have been the natural expectation of his parents and friends that he would soon produce a novel. Short stories had, indeed, more currency at the end of the nineteenth century than they have today; there were many more 'outlets' for them in magazines of respectable literary status. Nevertheless, the novel had established itself as the age's major form of imaginative writing, and it was almost taken for granted that the short story must necessarily be of lesser consequence; Henry James reflects this feeling when he describes himself, at the start of his own career in the 1870's, as 'bumping about, to acquire skill, in the shallow waters and sandy coves of the "short story"'. Already in India Kipling had been understood to be working on a novel of which the title was to be *Mother Maturin;* indeed in the summer of 1885 he declared that there existed 237 foolscap pages of it. For some reason these were left behind him in India, and shortly after reaching London he wrote to his parents asking that they be forwarded; he might, he thought, work up the material into something suitable for an English publisher. Nothing came of this; the manuscript was subsequently cannibalized in the interest of other writings, including *Kim* (1901), and after that it was probably destroyed. Now in London, during this fantastically productive and nervously exhausting year 1890, Kipling began and finished quite a different novel, *The Light that Failed.* It was when he was at work on it that Flo Garrard turned up again. The novel was already charting a recognizably autobiographical course—and Kipling at once thrust Flo straight into it. It is difficult to think of any other notable English novel, unless it be D. H. Lawrence's *Sons and Lovers*, which is so substantially created out of acutely painful experience actually being suffered by the writer within the period of its composition.

The Light that Failed set the critics a stiff problem almost from the start—and for a very odd reason. It appeared on the market in two distinct forms in rapid succession. In the first of these it is essentially a novelette: something a good deal shorter than even a short novel, and thus suitable for publishing (as in fact it was) within the covers of a single issue of a monthly magazine. Thus presented, it revealed as its main thread a sombre and troubled love story abruptly concluding with an almost unbelievably bad 'happy' ending. Within three months of this, the story appeared in book form in England, and proved both to be one-third longer and to have a tragic close. As a Preface, and above Kipling's signature, there was printed the following single sentence: 'This is the story of *The Light that Failed* as it was originally conceived by the Writer.'

One has almost to go back to the first publication of Shakspeare's *Sonnets* in 1609, and to their famous dedication to 'Mr. W. H.', to find anything equally enigmatic. 'Originally conceived' may, or may not, imply 'originally written'. And 'conceived by the Writer' may, or may not, carry the suggestion 'before it was altered or influenced by somebody else'. It does not even positively affirm that Kipling now prefers, or regards as definitive, the longer and tragic version which he thus introduces. How did this strange state of affairs come about? Mr. Carrington points the way to an answer when he remarks that: 'A study of Kipling's earlier work reveals *The Light that Failed* as a *pastiche* of extracts from his notebooks, strung together with an autobiographical motive which, here and there, is emphasized so strongly that the actual reminiscences intrude upon the feigned story.' Our inference must be that the novel was hastily run up in the course of that extraordinary year 1890, during which Kipling was also writing powerfully and prolifically in other forms—and during which, too, he was deeply involved in personal troubles which were to bring him near to nervous collapse. We must conclude that the supposed necessity of proving himself capable of being a real 'novelist' had got the better of his judgement; that he worked from hand to mouth; and that he arrived finally at a state in which he could be persuaded to make the most vulgar of concessions to meet the taste of both an English and an American magazine public. It is only fair to notice that this was something quite commonly done. Within a year of the first appearance of *The Light that Failed*, Thomas Hardy, a mature and established novelist of great integrity, was busy bowdlerizing *Tess of the D'Urbervilles* for magazine purposes.

It is certainly the longer and later-published version that we must consider, since it is always in this form that we meet the novel in subsequent authorized editions of Kipling's works. Here is how it opens:

> 'What do you think she'd do if she caught us? We oughtn't to have it, you know,' said Maisie.
>
> 'Beat me, and lock you up in your bedroom,' Dick answered, without hesitation. 'Have you got the cartridges?'

We are back, without a doubt, in the House of Desolation. But there are some differences. Dick Heldar is older than Black Sheep; he is at a public school where there are already smaller boys whom he can hit, when the spirit moves him, 'cunningly and with science'; he is distinguishably rather a tough character already. But in the holidays, when he returns to his cruel guardian Mrs. Jennings, he continues to allow her to cane him. This is an improbability, and it arises from the necessity of making the boy old enough to fall in love, in an adolescent fashion, with the girl. For the girl is no longer a sister; for the purposes of romantic development later, she is just a girl. The cartridges are for a revolver which Dick—again rather improbably—has been allowed to buy for seven shillings and sixpence. The revolver is there so that Maisie, firing it inexpertly, can nearly blind Dick. We find later that there is something symbolical in this incident. It is all that really happens in this brief glimpse of Dick Heldar's childhood.

We have to remember that Kipling almost certainly wrote this chapter before Flo Garrard turned up in his life again—but also that his first encounter with her had actually been at Lorne Lodge, of which she had been an inmate. Some readers feel that the childhood Maisie is more like Trix than Flo, and that it was the return of Flo to the scene in 1890 that determined much of the final course of the book. We cannot say much more than this; that the first chapter as we have it presages a fatal relationship of some sort between Dick and Maisie. If this were not so, the episode of the near-disaster with the revolver would be inept and inconsequent in a fashion inconceivable in Kipling.

We are now taken immediately to a view of Dick as a young man. He is a painter, possibly of genius, who has been roughing it about the world and picking up a living by doing honest, realistic and horrific sketches as a 'war artist'. Dick has really seen battle; Kipling, we may recall, had achieved much the same thing in his own medium—notably in 'The Drums of the Fore and Aft'—without ever having seen a gun fired in anger. Dick has done a number of things which we instinctively feel would not have been in Kipling's line: for instance, he has depicted, on a ship's rotten plates in brown, green and black paint, 'a sort of Negroid-Jewess-Cuban, with morals to match' and with 'the sea outside and unlimited love-making inside, and the fear of death atop of everything else'. If we pursue the autobiographical reference, we shall probably come to feel that Dick is a kind of dream-Kipling. Or, better, we may agree with Dr. J. M. S. Tompkins in her study of Kipling's work. Dick, despite the ramshackle structure in which he has his being, is the product of a certain artistic detachment and consideration; he is Kipling 'stripped of family and ballast'. Dick, as we learn in the first chapter, is an orphan. In Dick's image Kipling is taking a hard look at himself as he might have been, had he never known the Family Square.

Dick returns to England, and takes a set of rooms overlooking the Thames Embankment. His friends are war correspondents of a toughness equal to his own. He is having an immense success, and being pursued by editors and picture-dealers whom he holds in contempt and scorn. He despises aesthetes who 'talk about art and the state of their souls' (we remember 'who moo and coo with womenfolk about their blessed souls'). He sinks into a deep cynicism in which he is capable of replacing a sincere graphic statement of the horrors of war by a fudged-up version suitable for a sentimental public (we remember how this very novel is going to have alternative hard and soft endings). Mr. Carrington says, justly enough, that Dick Heldar is 'at once brutal and sentimental, a singularly unpleasant hero'. Yet nobody who has had much acquaintance with young writers and artists is unfamiliar with Dick in his essential lineaments; his bouts of ill nature, his self-absorption, his raging against commercial people whom he sees as intent to pervert and prostitute his talent: all these are to the life. Set Dick against Bernard Shaw's nearly contemporary portraits of a young painter or writer in the Dubidat of *The Doctor's Dilemma* or the Marchbanks of *Candida*, and Shaw's creations turn to printer's ink.

Upon this Dick Heldar, Maisie, his childhood's love, turns up again—accidentally, in the street. He is on the Embankment when

> . . . a shift of the same wind that had opened the fog drove across Dick's face the black smoke of a river-steamer at her berth below the wall. He was blinded for the moment, then spun round and found himself face to face with—Maisie.

But 'the years had turned the child to a woman'—and a 'New Woman' (as the type was soon to be called), sexually cold, capable only of a self-absorption hardly equalled by Dick's own, desperately exploiting, in the interest of a 'career', her wholly inadequate talent as a painter. Dick is quickly in the grip of a fatal passion, urged in vain. And it destroys him. Soon he is actually going blind—mysteriously, but as we know that the boy Kipling at Lorne Lodge had reason to fear that he might do. Dick makes a desperate return to a wholly masculine world, and manages to reach Egypt, where his finest work as a war artist has been done. And there, a blind man, he gets himself wantonly killed.

When we consider this story soberly we see that it is—like Hardy's *Jude the Obscure* or Lawrence's *Lady Chatterley's Lover*—a thoroughly bad novel which is at the same time the plain work of genius. Like these, it is a sick man's book—but, unlike these, a very young sick man's book. Its power comes from the irruption, for a time, of something always latent in Kipling: an almost magical fear and hatred of women—of women who are not good chaps, answering to nicknames like William and Ted.

Almost exactly a year after publishing the 'hard' version of *The Light that Failed*, Kipling was to be a married man.

CHAPTER SIX

VERMONT

THERE IS NO real mystery about Kipling's providing a sentimental—and ruthlessly inartistic—conclusion for *The Light that Failed* in its novelette form. The course must have been urged upon him, on commercial grounds, by a young American called Wolcott Balestier, who was in England at the time as the European representative of J. W. Lovell & Co., the firm contracted to publish the story in New York. This is an astonishing thing to have happened. Granted that Kipling during this period was as cynical as Dick Heldar is represented to be, he was yet the son of Lockwood Kipling, the nephew of Edward Burne-Jones, the 'nephew' too, in the family idiom, of William Morris, and himself an artist with an uncompromising sense of the ethics of art. Wolcott Balestier must have been a remarkable young man.

He was certainly a keen, and even pushing, man of business, looking forward to a successful career as a publisher's agent. He also had ambitions as a writer, and although he possessed little talent here, this, too, was to be relevant to Kipling's life. He had established himself in London in 1888, and at once commended himself to literary society in a remarkable way. He was a person of great charm. Henry James, the most stringent critic of his fellow-countrymen's manners abroad, became his enthusiastic admirer. So, in the course of 1890, did Kipling. At Balestier's suggestion, the two began collaborating on a rapidly run up romance, *The Naulahka, a Novel of East and West* (1892). The title conveys the essential idea: Kipling was to provide Indian scenes and Balestier American scenes; the two were to be strung together on a thread of melodramatic narrative concerning the theft of a fabulous jewel, the Naulahka, from an Indian Native State. Kipling wrote much of his part out of old travel notes. We are surprised to find him involved with such an artistic nullity. In fact, his warm regard for his recently made friend had intensified into something like complete devotion.

Meanwhile Balestier's social success in London continued, and soon his mother, two sisters, and younger brother arrived to share it. This bare statement holds a hint of absurdity which was not answered by the facts. The Balestiers were distinguished people, descended from Huguenot ancestors who had emigrated to America in the eighteenth century. One of them married a daughter of Paul Revere, and a later marriage connected them with the Wolcotts, an ancient New England family which had given three Governors to the State of Connecticut; there was another forebear who had signed the Declaration of Independence. Wolcott's Balestier grandfather, after a successful legal career in New York, settled near Brattleboro, a small country town in Vermont, and lived in a somewhat European style which did not pass unremarked by his rural neighbours—a pattern which was curiously to repeat itself, two generations on. In the Balestiers, then, Kipling encountered something new to him: a patrician strain in American society. He liked it very much.

That his interest in America continued is instanced in another episode in the crowded years 1890 and 1891. He was in a poor state of health and suffering from evident nervous exhaustion, and he had been urged by his doctor to take a long sea-voyage—at that time a favourite prescription in such a case. This he did not immediately do; instead, he accompanied a Macdonald uncle on a quick visit to another Macdonald uncle in the United States. The trip was an abortive one, since the American uncle died while they were at sea. Moreover, Kipling, conscious of his notoriety on the other side of the Atlantic, had travelled under an assumed name; this not very sensible expedient had been detected, and he himself returned to London rapidly and in some disgust.

Wolcott Balestier's mother and two sisters remained for some time in England; the younger brother Beatty, of whom more will be heard, had been hastily shipped home—apparently because he had been behaving with a cheerful lack of decorum on the London scene. In July Kipling spent some time with Wolcott and the three ladies in the Isle of Wight. In August he finally did set out on a voyage round the world. By this time, although it is not well documented, there was possibly some understanding between him and the elder of Wolcott's two sisters, Caroline, who was three years older than himself. At least his subsequent conduct must be considered highly impulsive, if this was not so. It is reported that his mother took one look at Carrie Balestier and said: 'That woman is going to marry our Ruddy.' But of the events leading up to Kipling's marriage only a few are certainly known.

Kipling held in some contempt the kind of aimless travellers known as globe-trotters, and now he appeared to be globe-trotting himself. But this was not so. For he was already a man with a mission.

We may recall how, at Westward Ho!, 'his strength had come to him' and there had been an end to being bullied. In his earliest weeks in London something of the same sort had happened; it was a period, he records, 'in which it seemed that I could push down walls, walk through ramparts and stride across rivers'. And so:

> Bit by bit, my original notion grew into a vast, vague conspectus . . . of the whole sweep and meaning of things and effort and origins throughout the Empire. I visualized it, as I do most ideas, in the shape of a semi-circle of buildings and temples projecting into a sea—of dreams.

There is a touch of the mysterious in this, but its main drift is clear. He was to be, in some sense, priest or prophet of the British Empire. Now he was seeing much more of that Empire at first-hand: South Africa, Australia, New Zealand, Ceylon, and regions of India which he had scarcely glimpsed before. Only the later part of the tour was hurried—for a reason to which we shall come.

Hitherto he had been inclined, simply as an accident of his upbringing, to see the Indian Empire as the norm of the imperial idea. India administered from above by authoritarian, incorruptible and devoted white civil servants; India enjoying the boon of the *pax Britannica* sustained by an English army progressively augmented by loyal and disciplined native troops, equally ready to put down communal discord and to repel the Russians at need: this had been the first centre of his faith and admiration. Now he was seeing the Empire in a fresh perspective, with India in some degree moving towards the periphery of the scene. The white Dominions had come into sharper focus; he was getting some notion of the economic basis of imperial policies; he was becoming aware of the key-importance of sea traffic and sea power. As one consequence of this, sailors were soon to fascinate him quite as much as soldiers had done.

Wolcott Balestier died suddenly during a visit to Dresden in the first week of December 1891 from an attack of typhoid. Kipling had reached his parents' home in Lahore, and there he received the news from Carrie Balestier by cable. She asked him to return. He left India at once, and was never to see it again. He arrived in London on 10th January 1892 after a very rapid journey. On 18th January he and Carrie were married. The occasion was virtually private, with only a handful of people present. Henry James gave away the bride, but didn't approve the match. He judged Carrie, indeed, 'remarkable in her force, acuteness, capacity, and courage'. But to his brother William James he wrote of her as 'a hard devoted capable little person whom I don't in the least understand his marrying'; and he added at once, after some mention of the 'dreary little wedding': 'Kipling strikes me personally as the most complete man of genius (as distinct from fine intelligence) that I have ever known.' Fine intelligence was Henry James's own endowment. But we must doubt whether it enabled him to see the marriage quite clearly. There was perhaps to be too much of Carrie's force and hardness to it in the end. But there was her courage as well. She was to employ it with unflinching devotion in the best interests, as she saw them, of the brilliant man who had been her brilliant brother's admiring friend. Kipling had found once more something that his inner nature deeply needed: the 'ballast' of protective affection that had hitherto come to him from the Family Square.

Kipling at the time of his marriage had about £2,000 in his bank account, and the near-certainty of a substantial income from royalties not far ahead. Carrie came of a family where comfortable fortunes were the rule, and she might expect to be an heiress in a small way one day. So there appeared to be no money problem facing the young couple, and they decided that their wedding-journey should take the generous form of a trip round the world, beginning, as was only proper, with a visit to Carrie's relations in Vermont, and including, equally correctly, a visit to Kipling's parents, still in Lahore; they might even manage to take in Robert Louis Stevenson in Samoa as well. The plan was put into effect rapidly, and they sailed for New York on 2nd February. Kipling finished *The Naulahka* on board.

They arrived at Brattleboro, Vermont, in the middle of February.

> As the light closed in, a little wooden town, white, cloaked, and dumb, slid past the windows, and the strong light of the car-lamps fell upon a sleigh (the driver furred and muffled to his nose) turning the corner of the street. . . . Thirty below freezing! It was inconceivable till one stepped out into it at midnight, and the first shock of that clear, still air took away the breath as does a plunge into sea-water. A walrus sitting on a woolpack was our host in his sleigh. . . . But for the jingle of the sleigh-bells the ride might have taken place in a dream, for there was no sound of hoofs upon the snow, the runners sighed a little now and again as they glided over an inequality, and all the sheeted hills round about were as dumb as death.

The walrus was Beatty Balestier, the same who had been sent hurriedly home from London. He was now a recently married man with an infant daughter, and possessed of a house and a seventy-acre farm on the family estate. Beatty—as Kipling was to discover to his cost—was a much-liked local character, being at once a Balestier (who were of the *élite* of Brattleboro) and a wild guy, given to intemperance, profanity, generosity and good fellowship. The Kiplings stayed for some days with the Beatty Balestiers, which was long enough for them to decide that they too must have a Brattleboro home. Beatty instantly offered them a plot of his own ground as a wedding present. Carrie, who had a talent for the prudent management of affairs which was to develop steadily, insisted on some legal formality there and then. Beatty conveyed about a seventh part of his land to them for a nominal sum, and there was some sort of restrictive covenant reserving to him certain grazing rights. When this was settled, and the infant daughter sufficiently admired, the Kiplings went happily on their way around the world. Japan in spring was delightful, and they tarried there for some weeks. Carrie's grandfather, an eminent international lawyer named Judge Peshine Smith, had been adviser to that

Mikado who had opened up his empire to the outside world; and the Kiplings as a consequence enjoyed a gratifying regard. Then a most disconcerting thing happened. The Oriental Banking Company failed, and Kipling's £2,000 vanished overnight. He was left with a bundle of steamship tickets and $100 on deposit in New York.

Back in London, the sagacious A. P. Watt would scarcely have regarded this as a crisis of the first order. *Barrack-Room Ballads* had been published and was proving enormously popular: in fact, it was to be reprinted some fifty times in the course of the succeeding thirty years. On this and other accounts, Kipling was already a certain winner. It was natural, however, that the young couple—thus all but stranded in Japan, and with a first child on the way—should take alarm; and natural that they should make a bee line back to Brattleboro, where the Balestiers were people of substance. Once more they were sheltered by the Beatty Balestiers, and then accommodated with a hired man's house for $10 a month. In September this seemed about right, for Watt's cheque was for $150. In October it has made a modest rise to $260. November brought $3,888. This in itself was far from being a fortune. But Kipling never had to think about money again.

Kipling had taken great satisfaction in all the small contrivances through which he insured that 'Bliss Cottage' should be tolerably comfortable for a mother and child through a New England winter. And in it his daughter Josephine was born 'in three foot of snow on the night of 29th December 1892'—the day before his own birthday and two days before Carrie's. It seemed, somehow, a good omen. Whatever had been the obscure emotional currents at play in bringing about his marriage, he was happy now. He decided to settle in Vermont. It would be his base for whatever else lay in store.

This may be judged a strange resolution on the part of a man who had been revolted by what he judged the crudities of American public and private life; who had announced his disapproval loudly and discourteously; and who had experienced 'joy' on perceiving that the fortifications of San Francisco could be demolished by a couple of British gunboats. Recalling that Carrie Kipling's was a dominating personality, we may suppose that the resolution to build a substantial house in Vermont (which is what the Kiplings now began to do) was predominantly hers. But there is no real evidence that this was so. However passionately Kipling was a citizen of the British Empire, he had never yet become quite comfortably an Englishman. And it was not merely the natural beauty and strongly accented climate of Vermont that enchanted and stimulated him. America stood for many things which it was native in him to admire: mere largeness and multifariousness and untapped power—but always, too, and for everybody, the sharp wholesome challenge of a hard day's work ahead. He found, also, a social structure to which he instinctively responded: one in which gentle and simple were still sufficiently distinguished not to disconcert an upper-middle-class Britisher as he went around; but in which, again, men were readily brought in ease and comradeship together at the call of constructive labour before common problems. It is quite accurate to say that Kipling fell in love with Vermont. The shock must have been very great when he (and his American wife) finally fell into grave error there.

The house was to be named 'Naulakha'—which gives the correct, as the title of the romance gives an incorrect, spelling of the word. Beatty, still abounding in cheerful hospitality, and a great contriver of parties and dances, handled much of the work; and it was probably as a consequence of this that his sister came rather rapidly to a sharpened perception that her brother was not a satisfactory person, particularly where money was concerned. He was not dishonest about it, only regardless—which seemed to Carrie just as bad. Beatty, whose livelihood was now coming largely from the Naulakha enterprise, found himself required to go to his sister for a dollar's commission on this, or two dollars twenty-five for that. Thus treated as a boy, he let bad feeling develop.

The person most at fault here was undoubtedly Kipling himself. The Balestiers (unlike the Macdonalds) were rather given to family frictions, and here was just that, developing under his nose. Had he taken Naulakha and Beatty in hand together, all might have been well. Instead, he went off on a trip to Canada with his father, now retired from India and embarking upon a vigorous and much-travelling old age. When he returned, the house was ready for occupation, and greatly delighted him. It had one notable feature, to be reduplicated in essentials wherever the Kiplings subsequently lived.

Kipling's study had only one entrance, through a room occupied by his wife. There Carrie would sit at a desk, ordering her domestic affairs, and guarding her husband against all possibility of intrusion. He could remain undisturbed for as long as he liked: sometimes, perhaps, for rather longer. And his father, untiring in the exercise of one or another of his crafts, carved a text on the study chimney-piece. It read: 'The Night cometh when No Man can Work.' In acknowledgement of this, Kipling entitled his next collection of stories *The Day's Work*. The text was, of course, very much *his* text. But we have to suppose that Carrie approved of it too.

This was in the summer of 1893. Kipling's attachment to Vermont did not wholly allay a certain restlessness of which we are regularly conscious in him. Early in 1894 there was a trip to Bermuda; then a return of a few weeks to Brattleboro (where Beatty was found to be more in debt than ever); after that a trip to England, where the Kiplings (without their infant daughter, who did not share in these voyages) spent three months in the Wiltshire Downs, close to the place where Lockwood and Alice Kipling had now made their home. There was talk of building a holiday cottage by the sea, and it appears to have been Carrie who turned this idea down. Kipling himself, though in many ways a man of tenacious purposes, did possess something of the volatility of the artist. He was now back in the close society of his beloved parents, and certainly aware that association with his father regularly strengthened the sensitiveness of his own work. The growing solidity of his reputation, moreover, had given him a surer stance in relation to English society. It may well be that he was now disposed to rethink the whole proposal to lead a preponderantly expatriate life. Certainly his feelings about America and the Americans were turning ambivalent again. For it was now that he wrote the lurkingly ill-natured story 'An Error in the Fourth Dimension' (*The Day's Work*).

There is a whole category of Kipling stories in which we are invited to be very much amused by the spectacle of a dislikeable person being in some way outrageously humiliated. This story veers too much in that direction to be wholly successful in its own kind—which Henry James would have called Comedy of the International Situation. But it is exceedingly funny—and, moreover, it has a further, and odd, claim upon our attention.

In a topsy-turvy fashion, it is like a work of prophesy. We can read it, that is to say, as an ironical inversion of something soon to be happening in Vermont.

We begin with a rather sympathetic portrait of an expatriate American millionaire, Wilton Sargent. He has inherited from his father controlling interests in several thousand miles of railway track, and sees no reason why he should himself go to an office daily, rather than cultivate fine tastes and liberal pursuits; 'so he fled, and they howled behind him that he was an unpatriotic Anglomaniac, born to consume fruits, one totally lacking in public spirit'. Sargent does not find living in England altogether easy. 'The impenetrability of this regulated life irritated him, and he strove to learn something of the human side of these people. He retired baffled, to be trained by his menials.' So long as he maintains this posture of observant and due humility, all is well; he is accepted. Nevertheless he is at risk, for 'there is room for an infinity of mistakes when a man begins to take liberties with his nationality'.

At this point, Kipling, as narrator, enters the story. He has been urgently invited by Sargent to his large country house, Holt Hangars. It turns out that a most bewildering thing has happened. Sargent has had occasion to visit London in a hurry (it was a matter of authenticating an Egyptian scarab—for he has all sorts of cultivated interests), and since one of England's mainline railways ran at the foot of his forty-acre lawn he had simply ordered his butler to go down and signal to the next train to stop. The butler had done so—resourcefully employing the red flag from the ninth hole of his employer's private golf course. The train—it proved to be one of the crack express trains of England—had duly stopped, but Sargent's attempt to board it had not been appreciated. In fact there had been a fight, Sargent had spent a night in a police cell, and been fined forty shillings by a magistrate next morning.

But that has not been the end of the matter. The Railway Company has been threatening Sargent with a civil action; his reasonable suggestion that their President should drop down to talk the matter over has been rejected; there has been a great deal of correspondence, with Sargent always declining to bring in his solicitor; now there has come the baffling suggestion that between the railway line and himself he should put up a fourteen-foot wall, crowned with bottle-glass. When Kipling hears this he has a glimpse of the truth, and it fills him 'with pure joy'. The Railway Company has come to the inevitable conclusion that Sargent must be mad. Only a lunatic, after all, could think of flagging down an English express train. On this basis a substantial farcical situation is built up, and the story concludes good-naturedly enough.

But 'An Error in the Fourth Dimension' is by no means good-natured all through. The story's essence is the comedy inherent in Anglo-American mutual incomprehension, and it must fail as soon as the balance of its sympathies is weighted on one side. For the most part Kipling here manœuvres very well, and Wilton Sargent gives as good as he gets. But, every now and then, the picture turns ugly; under stress, Sargent's Americanness is described as 'beginning to ooze out all over', and his voice rises 'to the high, throaty crow of his breed when they labour under excitement'. This is unpleasant, and it has offended some sophisticated Americans, including Mr. Edmund Wilson. Yet along with it, in the descriptive snatches depicting Sargent's native background, we can detect in the writing a note of positive nostalgia for the American scene. Kipling, as much as Wilton Sargent, doesn't quite know where he stands.

The return to Naulakha was made in August 1894, and it ended in disaster just two years later. They were years of continued domestic contentment, crowned by the birth of a second daughter, Elsie, in February 1896; and marked, too, by the inception of several notable friendships: with Theodore Roosevelt, and at Harvard with Charles Eliot Norton and his circle. But American life was changing—and, in Kipling's view, not for the better. He had founded his notions of it in terms of the New England tradition, and this he now believed to be vanishing. A visit to the White House of President Cleveland disturbed him very much; the spectacle was 'awful, inexpressible, incredible'. He was full of the direst forebodings (as were his sympathetic friends, the Brahmins of Boston) when relations between Britain and America took a critical turn in the border dispute over British Guiana, and there seemed even to be the possibility of war. And then relations with Beatty took a critical turn too.

There had been trouble over the construction of a tennis-court. There was more trouble over a piece of land which Beatty claimed to have retained the right to mow, but which Carrie (who was getting increasingly large ideas) had begun to turn into a formal garden. Eventually Beatty went bankrupt. Carrie, very foolishly, undertook to support his daughter for a year on condition that Beatty himself and his wife went away. Kipling should certainly have put a stop to all this. Brattleboro had seen him turn from a penniless English scribbler to one of the wealthiest men in the district—this in an astonishingly short space of time. It was unseemly and injudicious to have his wife quarrelling over petty sums with her own brother, particularly as that brother's character and temperament, although no doubt variously reprehensible, were such as to have largely established him in the affectionate regard of the place. Actually it was Kipling, and not Carrie, who made the worst mistakes.

Kipling took great satisfaction in yarning, on his own 'copy'-hunting terms, with all and sundry in Brattleboro, but at the same time he was extremely jealous of his personal privacy. The Kiplings had come to be judged rather too stand-offish and superior, and this effect was enhanced by some aspects of their style of living. They had imported from New York a coachman who wore livery and was known to have been in the employment of an English lord. A cook had departed in dudgeon because of the caps Carrie required her to wear. This sort of thing, and still more the worsening relations with Beatty, were not merely matter of small-town gossip; concerning as they did a man who had made himself notorious by stringent criticism of American institutions, they were news. Reporters came to the house and lurked in the highways. Kipling expressed himself forcefully about this. It was an explosive situation, and common prudence ought to have prompted him to conciliate Beatty. Instead, he allowed months to go by without exchanging a word with him. Then, one day, Kipling went for a bicycle ride, took a tumble at the foot of a hill, and picked himself up to find Beatty, apparently drunk, brandishing a whip at him and shouting incoherent accusations of slander. There was an altercation in the course of which Beatty threatened to blow out his brother-in-law's 'goddam brains'; Kipling pointed out that this might involve him in some trouble with the law; and Beatty shouted, 'Do you dare to threaten me, you little bastard?', and drove off.

Kipling was good at handling drunken violence in short stories; he could make a very funny business of it. But when the real thing erupted on him like this, he was much disturbed. He must also have been put in actual bodily fear, for the next morning he caused Beatty to be arrested on a charge of threatening him with murder. This was on a Saturday. The case was adjourned over the week-end, and Beatty released on bail. He went off ('with pure joy' would have been Kipling's phrase) to the telegraph office, and Brattleboro had its brief moment of national—indeed, international—fame. There were more than forty reporters in court when the case was resumed on the Tuesday. Kipling, the one witness for the prosecution, was kept on the stand all day. The local lawyers, delighted with their unprecedented press-gallery, excelled themselves in exhibiting the whole episode in a ludicrous light. Beatty was eventually bound over for trial at the next appointed session of the County Court. Kipling had to recognize that the whole humiliating performance would have to be gone through again. In fact, the case never came to trial, since the Kiplings left America before it could come up. It is very possible that this was an intention which had been strengthening in them from some time back. But again Kipling had to face something. It could be represented, not implausibly, that he had broken and run for it. And, in his case, there were no drummers to inspire a rally.

It is occasionally suggested that far too much has been made of the effect upon Kipling of this family feud in Vermont; that it was neither the prime reason for his leaving the United States nor of any enduring significance in his mind. But on his last day at Naulakha, Mr. Carrington tells us, two ladies came to call. 'There are only two places in the world,' he told them, 'where I want to live—Bombay and Brattleboro. And I can't live at either.' This certainly indicates that he was extremely upset. Nevertheless, had his experience of the United States ended here, it could well have been preserved for the uses of comedy, broadly speaking. Unfortunately, when Kipling made one further visit two years later, the result was the first of two domestic tragedies which he was to experience.

The winter of 1898 was spent in South Africa, the family (which now included an infant son, John, born in the summer of 1897) setting sail on 8th January. This was to become their habit for a number of years, and as a result of it, and of a consequent association with Cecil Rhodes and others, South Africa was established as a principal focus of Kipling's political interests. In the immediately succeeding winter, however, they determined to go to New York: Kipling judged that a visit might help to clear up further copyright disputes, and Carrie wished to see her mother. It was perhaps this latter motive that carried the day when Alice Kipling tried to dissuade her son from making the journey with young children at so bleak a season of the year. But the eldest child, Josephine, certainly looked forward to the trip; she often spoke about Naulakha with longing, and was declared by her father to be altogether a little American.

The passage was exceptionally stormy, and at the end of it the Kiplings had a two-hour wait in a draughty custom-house; by the time they reached the Hotel Grenoble in West 56th Street it had become evident that the two little girls were ill. A few days later, Carrie too succumbed, and not long after her recovery Kipling himself fell very ill indeed. The chief family news was that Beatty, aware of their arrival but not, presumably, of their misfortunes, had, through the press, announced to the world at large that he proposed at once to sue his brother-in-law for $50,000 on the score of malicious prosecution. Elsie recovered quickly, and the baby John was said to have no more than a touch of bronchitis. Josephine and her father remained in grave danger, and eventually Kipling's life was despaired of. The public response to this private calamity was astonishing; prayers were said in New York churches, and outside the Hotel Grenoble crowds stood silent in the street. Perhaps because there was no major international news at the time, the world's press focused its attention upon two sick men: Rudyard Kipling and Pope Leo XIII. Both survived. Josephine Kipling died on 6th March, and it was a long time before Kipling was strong enough to be told the news. It is said that Carrie, returning from her daughter's funeral to her husband's sick-bed, and suddenly realizing that she was dressed, after the fashion of the time, in deep mourning, snatched up a coloured shawl and threw it round herself just in time. It is clear that, throughout this dreadful ordeal, she behaved with unflinching fortitude and resolution. Henry James (who now wrote a couple of hysterical letters) had called her, among other things, 'poor concentrated Carrie', and Lockwood Kipling (upon an early acquaintance) described her as 'a good man spoiled'. It can be said that, like William, she survived her ordeal very much a conqueror.

Kipling's recovery brought him messages of congratulation from all over the world. There was one from John Ruskin and one from the German Kaiser.

Kipling was to retain many correspondents in the United States, Theodore Roosevelt being chief among them. But family ties weakened with the death of Carrie's mother in 1919 —an event which revealed that much of her capital had been used up in supporting Beatty. In the Kipling household Beatty's name was tabu, so that Elsie and John grew up scarcely knowing that they had an uncle in America. Beatty died in the same year as Kipling, 1936. It is said that, at the end, he regretted the injury he had done his sister and her family, and wished that they could have been reconciled.

CHAPTER SEVEN

NEW HORIZONS

CAPTAINS COURAGEOUS (1897) is the most substantial direct product of the Vermont period. It could not have been written but for the help of the family doctor, James Conland, with whom Kipling struck up a warm friendship at the time of the birth of his second child. As a young man Conland had served with the fishing fleets off the Grand Banks; he had many stories to tell; the two men made expeditions to the old T-wharf of Boston Harbour, and to Gloucester, which was still the centre of the fishing industry. It was a new world for Kipling to master, and he 'revelled in profligate abundance of detail —not necessarily for publication but for the joy of it'. Nothing came amiss:

> Charts we got—old and new—and the crude implements of navigation such as they used off the Banks, and a battered boat-compass, still a treasure with me. (Also, by pure luck I had sight of the first sickening uprush and vomit of iridescent coal-dusted water into the hold of a ship, a crippled iron hulk, sinking at her moorings.)

Kipling was soon working—it seems with a concentration exceptional even in him—at a romance based upon this new material. It was to be his only book in which the characters and setting are wholly American.

The actual story does not suggest great concentration, since it may without much unfairness be described as a typical Kipling fable of the more superficial sort. Fifteen-year-old Harvey Cheyne is the spoilt son of a railway millionaire who is presumably too busy to bother with him, and he is dragged about America (and is now on his way to be dragged about Europe) by a doting and foolish mother. We meet him as he enters the smoking-room of an Atlantic liner, 'a half-smoked cigarette hanging from one corner of his mouth'. 'His pasty yellow complexion did not show well on a person of his years, and his look was a mixture of irresolution, bravado, and very cheap smartness.' Fortunately this 'hotel child' (as Henry James named boys of Harvey's stamp) is washed overboard, and picked up by a dory from the schooner *We're Here*, so that he finds himself lying on a pile of half-dead fish. This is salutary in itself, and it happens on page six. On page fifteen, indeed, he is accusing his rescuers of stealing the one hundred and thirty-four dollars which is left of his month's pocket-money. But Harvey is a good boy at heart, and discovers the fact at the cost of only one blow. By page twenty-five he is virtually saved, and on page one hundred and ninety-one he is restored to the inspection of his father, who is 'well used to judging men':

> He distinctly remembered an unsatisfied dough-faced youth who took delight in 'calling down the old man' and reducing his mother to tears—such a person as adds to the gaiety of public rooms and hotel piazzas where the ingenuous young of the wealthy play with or revile the bell-boys. But this well-set-up fisher youth did not wriggle, looked at him with eyes steady, clear, and unflinching, and spoke in a tone distinctly, even startlingly, respectful. There was that in his voice, too, which seemed to promise that the change might be permanent, and that the new Harvey had come to stay.

All this has been achieved by a little roughing it. There is, of course, truth in the fable, as there is truth in all Kipling's fables; and innumerable popular stories and films have been concocted in imitation of it. But there is something a little perfunctory, or at least sketchy, about its embodiment in *Captains Courageous*. Kipling's energy is really being directed elsewhere. Harvey Cheyne is something other than an individual made to illustrate a 'tough' theory of eduation. In his unredeemed state he, and his parents with him, represent something that Kipling believed he saw emerging in American society and knew he didn't like. Over against it he is setting an older and simpler order, in which he believed the nation's virtue to reside. Ever since its first appearance, the book has been acclaimed as an astonishing triumph of imaginative reporting, for its seascapes and the technicalities of the fishing operations are brought utterly alive. But Kipling's further intention is at least hinted in *Something of Myself:*

> Yet the book was not all reporterage. I wanted to see if I could catch and hold something of a rather beautiful localized American atmosphere that was already beginning to fade.

Essentially, it is a moral atmosphere that is in question. And Kipling is taking immense pains (to be seen, for example, in his endeavour to master dialect) to paint convincingly and movingly a small group of characters whom he wants us to judge at their proper worth. The book is, after a fashion, his gift to Vermont and to America.

In several of Kipling's sea stories we shall find satisfaction only if prepared to be much more interested in ships than in the men who sail them. Indeed, a letter written in 1895 declares uncompromisingly that 'marine engines and such like' will probably be his next concern in fiction. The promise is drastically fulfilled in two stories in *The Day's Work:* 'The Ship that Found Herself' and 'The Devil and the Deep Sea'. The first describes the maiden voyage across the Atlantic of a twenty-five hundred ton cargo-steamer, the *Dimbula*, and it consists almost entirely of dialogue. But although the Captain, Chief Engineer, and owner's daughter are allowed a few words, most of the discussion is conducted by the various parts of the ship:

> As soon as she met the lift in the open water, she naturally began to talk. If you lay your ear to the side of the cabin the next time you are in a steamer, you will hear hundreds of little voices in every direction, thrilling and buzzing, and whispering and popping, and gurgling and sobbing and squeaking exactly like a telephone in a thunder-storm. Cast iron, as a rule, says very little; but mild steel plates and wrought-iron, and ribs and beams that have been much bent and welded and riveted, talk continuously.

They talk continuously here, ending up with some pardonable boasting as, much battered, the *Dimbula* sails past a row of pompous liners in the Port of New York. Kipling applied this curious animism to other mechanisms besides steam-ships—and most famously, perhaps, to a railway-engine in a story called '.007' (*The Day's Work*). Henry James was one who did not kindle to such enterprises; and he thus described Kipling's progress:

> He has come down steadily from the simple in subject to the more simple—from the Anglo-Indians to the natives, from the natives to the Tommies, from the Tommies to the quadrupeds, from the quadrupeds to the fish, and from the fish to the engines and screws.

It is the engines and screws which are most prominent in 'The Devil and the Deep Sea'. Here the *Aglaia* (only she has passed under a dozen other names), while peacefully engaged in pearl-stealing in a very large way, has her engines wrecked by a sighting shot from a gun-boat of the foreign power in whose waters this routine piracy is being conducted. In the end the crew get the *Aglaia* under steam again—although in a crazy fashion—and triumphantly scuttle her in a harbour-mouth in such a way that the gun-boat is bound to be in collision with the submerged hulk and sink. Formally, therefore, 'The Devil and the Deep Sea' is a story of revenge—a theme to which, in the view of some readers, Kipling is more addicted than is wholly agreeable. But in this story the revenge is merely touched in as a flourish at the end, and almost the whole narrative is devoted to a minutely circumstantial account of the various technical processes involved in the repairs. We cannot avoid feeling that Kipling is shamelessly showing off. But he does so with a captivating impetus and *élan*, so that we are more likely, on the whole, to be excited than bored. 'Marine engines and such like' *did* excite Kipling himself, and he has the power to pass his excitement on.

A broader interest attaches to 'Bread upon the Waters', another story in *The Day's Work*—and very decidedly yet another story of revenge. It tells of a ship's engineer (a Scot, as Kipling appears firmly convinced that all ship's engineers are), McPhee. He has been dismissed after twenty years' service because he has declined to join in certain dishonest practices of his owners. Aided by the guile of another, and friendly, ship-owner, he contrives to rescue as a derelict (which means to enormous profit) one of his former employers' freighters. Everything depends here upon the bravura, speed and assurance with which Kipling's brush flies over its marine canvas. There are scarcely half a dozen of his stories which are as brilliantly entertaining. Beyond entertainment, we are not here carried.

Read as a group, Kipling's stories about ships and sailors probably appear most striking on the score of their descriptive writing. It is astonishing that a man whose main experience of the sea (apart from one or two uncomfortable trips as a guest of naval commanders on board cruisers and destroyers) came to him as a first-class passenger on Cunard, P. & O., or Union Castle liners should write with so nautical an air, and create such a remarkable variety of seascapes. But in another direction in which he began to extend his range in the early 1890's he was to go further. This was in his exploitation of the supernatural. He was to write some of his most mature masterpieces in this kind.

The interest had been with him from his earliest days as an author, for some of the *Schoolboy Lyrics* (so rashly printed by his proud parents) deal in ghostly manifestations. We have seen something of the sort, too, in 'The Mark of the Beast'. 'The Phantom Rickshaw', a very early and not particularly successful tale, also embodies it, and is of interest because Kipling singles out this story as the first in which what he calls his 'personal Daemon' (itself a conception tinged with the supernatural) was at work. More effective had been 'At the End of the Passage' (*Life's Handicap*), which begins as a wholly realistic and very powerfully realized description of the gradual nervous collapse of an Englishman obliged by duty to live in unbearable conditions through the ordeal of an Indian summer on the plains. Later in his career, Kipling was to be fascinated by what he called the 'breaking strain': the point at which suffering produces ultimate despair, and ultimate despair a vision of absolute evil and of hell. In this story Hummil passes from insomnia to hallucination; and when he is found dead, 'in the staring eyes was written terror beyond the expression of any pen'. But what has thus been revealed to Hummil in the end is precisely *not* hallucination; he has really *seen* something the image of which has lingered and been recorded by a camera:

> After breakfast they smoked a pipe in silence to the memory of the dead. Then Spurstow said absently—

''Tisn't in medical science.'

'What?'

'Things in a dead man's eye.'

'For goodness' sake leave that horror alone!' said Lowndes. 'I've seen a native die of pure fright when a tiger chivied him. I know what killed Hummil.'

'The deuce you do! I'm going to try to see.' And the doctor retreated into the bathroom with a Kodak camera. After a few minutes there was the sound of something being hammered to pieces, and he emerged, very white indeed.

The idea here is perhaps a little too bizarre for full effectiveness, but it is based on a sound instinct to permit the irruption of the mysterious and unknown only into a familiar world which the writer is in a position to depict with absolute confidence and verisimilitude. This holds, very notably, of two stories in *The Day's Work*: 'The Bridge-Builders' and 'The Brushwood Boy'.

The first opens upon a situation which may remind us of 'William the Conqueror'. Two Englishmen, Findlayson and his assistant Hitchcock, are engineers entrusted with the task of building a bridge over the Ganges, and they are addressing themselves to this with all the efficiency and devotion to be expected of white *sahibs*. The native workmen are unreliable; they lose their heads in any crisis and take to useless shouting; and one such muddle results in Hitchcock finding himself with a broken arm—but he buttons it up in his coat and, after coming out of a faint, continues to direct operations for four hours. From some remote height above Findlayson and Hitchcock the Government of India issue idiotic instructions for altering the specifications of the bridge—much as if it were something one could cut out of paper. Thus isolated between uncomprehending superiors and a labour force without a single man whom they 'would have honoured by working as remorselessly as they worked themselves' they struggle on. In point of personal advancement little or nothing will come of it—perhaps a minor decoration at the end of a career. Still, they have their job to do.

This is very familiar Kipling, and so is the developing situation, when the Ganges comes down in flood at an unpredictable season, and the unfinished bridge has to be protected as well as may be against the advancing threat. Desperate measures are taken, and Kipling describes them with minute and convincing particularity. We might be reading a yarn written for civil engineers by a civil engineer. Then something happens which changes the whole focus of the story. Findlayson, utterly exhausted and having eaten nothing for many hours, accepts 'as a good guard against fever' some opium tablets from one of his men. Having fallen under the power of the drug, he is swept down the river and wrecked on an island. There—as a matter of hallucination, we must suppose—he finds himself witnessing a coming together of the ancient gods of India. The Goddess of the Ganges (she has the form of a crocodile) speaks of the indignity imposed upon her by Findlayson's bridge; Indra makes light of this, for in the sight of the gods so puny a thing can endure not long enough to be regarded. Indeed, the gods themselves must pass, Krishna says, since they are but figments within the dream of Brahm. In the latter part of this story we are likely to find the gods far too talkative—but of Indian gods this is to be expected, after all. The sharp juxtaposition of two visions, one wholly practical and finite, the other mystical and indefinite, is not merely extremely effective. It comes to us as an internal debate between two Kiplings: the Kipling who was the son of the *raj*, convinced that bridges must be built even if it needs the 'whipping powers' which Hitchcock is armed with as 'a magistrate of the third class'; and the Kipling who was Lockwood Kipling's son and therefore to be able to write *Kim*—a man deeply reverencing the immemorial spirit of India. And, more than this, 'The Bridge-Builders' is in fact making a statement of wide philosophical generality; a statement which Kipling's greatest poem was to make too:

> Far-called, our navies melt away;
>   On dune and headland sinks the fire:
> Lo, all our pomp of yesterday
>   Is one with Nineveh and Tyre!
> Judge of the Nations, spare us yet,
> Lest we forget—lest we forget!

In *A Passage to India* E. M. Forster's least amiable Anglo-Indians jocularly give the name of 'bridge party' to any gathering designed—fatuously, as they think—to bring Indians and English together. Recalling this, we may feel that a certain resonance is carried even by the title of Kipling's story.

'The Brushwood Boy' is another story of 'double vision', but it is at once more subtle and more disconcerting. Its hero is called Georgie Cottar. We are given a brief glimpse of him as a child of three, waking from some terrifying dream, and an equally brief glimpse of him three years later, when his dreams are repeating themselves with variations, and thus building up a region and a life of their own. Then we learn that 'ten years at an English public school do not encourage dreaming'. But Georgie is captain of games and captain of the school; at Sandhurst he gains the Sword of Honour and is commissioned as a subaltern 'in a first-class line regiment'. He is a superb subaltern and soon a superb Captain; later he is decorated for bravery, and becomes the youngest Major in the British Army. He comes home on a year's leave, and we find that he is what all good Englishmen would wish to be: the son and heir of a substantial country gentleman. His parents adore him, since he has returned honourable, chaste, and covered in glory. Old family retainers gather round and admire; he rides and fishes and shoots. He has long confidential talks with his mother when he has gone to bed ('as mother and son should, if there is to be any future for our empire'); and when he gets up she shows him off to the best society in the county. His father takes him up to London and parades him before awed old Army cronies at his club. And so on, and so on—until, before this remorseless exhibition of a straight Kipling-type paragon, the nerve of the reader is ready to break. Here, quite flatly, is Kipling's dream-hero. He even finds a dream girl, and marries her. But she is a rather special sort of dream girl—for she turns out to have been the principal figure in Georgie's dreams ever since she was a child. And *he* has always been in *her* dreams. In fact they share an enormous dream-world in its minutest detail. And it is a dream-world against the infinite dimensions and mysterious significance of which Georgie's exemplary waking life reveals itself as being as flat as paper. Or say rather that, although Georgie's career is truly honourable and enviable in quite a solid three-dimensional universe, he has access to some other universe where a further dimension is added. It is good to live in an English country house. It is possible to live somewhere else as well.

Some readers feel that this story is fundamentally inept; others, that the writer has in some way overreached himself in it, so that it 'doesn't come off'. It is certainly not the work of a naïve craftsman, or of a shallow mind.

Kipling, as we shall see, had a strong personal motive for distrusting 'spiritualism', or even the intellectually somewhat better-accredited activity known as 'psychical research'. But he was never to deny the existence of such mysterious frontiers of the human mind as 'The Brushwood Boy' intimates. They are explored in two related, and equally brilliant stories, 'The Finest Story in the World' and 'Wireless'.

In the first of these (*Many Inventions*, 1893) we meet Charlie Mears, a twenty-year-old London bank clerk, ill-educated and essentially commonplace, but with an ambition to be a writer which recommends him to the sympathy of the narrator, whom we may take to be Kipling. Charlie falls into the way of bringing along his latest compositions for criticism (by which he means praise), and he also takes to doing some writing in Kipling's rooms, since it is an unprofitable and eccentric activity which his mother disapproves of. Charlie has no notion of the gap between conception and achievement, 'seeing all that he intended to do so clearly that he esteemed it already done'. But after a time it becomes clear that Charlie has a halting and mysterious command of something not at all commonplace; something that *would* make 'the finest story in the world', if only he could get at it other than in the 'horrible sentences that he purposed to use'. He thinks that it ought to be called 'The Story of a Ship'. In fragments of his conversation Charlie shows that this ship is utterly real to him. It is a three-decked galley, rowed by slaves and 'Can't you imagine,' he asks, 'the sun-light just squeezing through between the handle and the hole and wobbling about as the ship moves?' Numerous other glimpses follow:

> 'When a man dies at his oar on that deck he isn't thrown overboard, but cut up in his chains and stuffed through the oar-hole in little pieces.'
>
> 'Why?' I demanded amazed, not so much at the information as the tone of command in which it was flung out.
>
> 'To save trouble and to frighten the others. It needs two

overseers to drag a man's body up to the top deck; and if the men at the lower-deck oars were left alone, of course they'd stop rowing and try to pull up the benches by all standing up together in their chains.'

'You've a most provident imagination. Where have you been reading about galleys and galley-slaves?'

'Nowhere that I remember. I row a little when I get the chance.'

Soon Charlie produces something even more startling: some 'scratches' that have come to him oddly while he was thinking over the story: 'the stuff the men might be supposed to scratch on the oars with the edges of their handcuffs'. Charlie says the scratches are 'great nonsense', but that he supposes they mean 'I'm beastly tired'. Kipling takes the scratches to an authority on Greek antiquities at the British Museum, who declares that they are corrupt Greek, the work of an extremely illiterate person, and may be translated: 'I have been—many times—overcome with weariness in this particular employment.' This incident can be seen to have the same function in 'The Finest Story in the World' as has the business of the Kodak in 'At the End of the Passage'; it affords objective evidence of there being some supernatural, or paranormal, element in play. In fact, Charlie Mears is recalling in snatches experiences which have befallen him in a previous life on earth. Nor are his memories of this kind confined to the Greek period; he can recall, too, something of 'some desperate adventure of the Vikings', and 'Thorfin Karlsefne's sailing to Wineland, which is America, in the ninth or tenth century'. Just when the narrator believes himself to be on the verge of great discoveries, invisible doors close upon these strange perspectives which Charlie commands. Fatally, he has fallen in love. 'Charlie,' the last sentence of the story tells us, 'had tasted the love of woman that kills remembrance, and the finest story in the world would never be written.' We feel Kipling's lurking antagonism to women to be at work here; he is expressing the notion—which Bernard Shaw was later to make much of in *Man and Superman*—that there is something incompatible between the demands made on a man by art and sexual love, or at least by art and domesticity. It is a persuasion elsewhere expressed and generalized by Kipling in a single trenchant line:

He travels the fastest who travels alone.

But this doctrine is no part of the essential excellence of 'The Finest Story in the World', which consists rather in the power of Kipling's historical imagination. It is really Kipling who has been in the Greek galley and the Danish ship, and who is therefore able to provide Charlie with the very words which appear to bring us vivid and concrete sensuous impressions from a remote past.

The somewhat later story, 'Wireless' (*Traffics and Discoveries*, 1904), is built on a very similar theme: the breaking in upon normal consciousness of inexplicable or irrational matter in a manner disturbing to our conventional ideas of the human mind in its temporal relations. Just as Charlie Mears has never learnt the Greek alphabet so another commonplace young man, Shaynor, has never heard of John Keats. Perhaps this is not surprising, since he is an ill-educated (and consumptive) apothecary's assistant in a chemist's shop at the sea-side. We meet him there on a cold winter's night; indeed, as he himself says, a bitter cold night. The game birds hung outside a poulterer's next door look cold too, despite their feathers:

> 'They ought to take these poultry in—all knocked about like that,' said Mr. Shaynor. 'Doesn't it make you feel fair perishing? See that old hare! The wind's nearly blowing the fur off him.'

But the inside of the shop holds a hint of the exotic and opulent —although merely on the strength of what is quite usual in old-fashioned chemist's shops:

> There was a confused smell of orris, Kodak films, vulcanite, tooth-powder, sachets, and almond-cream in the air. . . . Electric lights, set low down in the windows before the tunbellied Rosamond jars, flung inward three monstrous daubs of red, blue, and green, that broke into kaleidoscopic lights on the faceted knobs of the drug-drawers, the cut-glass scent flagons, and the bulbs of the sparklet bottles. They flushed the white-tiled floor in gorgeous patches; splashed along the nickel-silver counter-rails, and turned the polished

> mahogany counter-panels to the likeness of intricate grained marbles—slabs of porphyry and malachite.

A girl whose name turns out to be Fanny Brand comes and takes Shaynor for a short walk 'round by St. Agnes'. On his return, he attempts to relieve his breathing by burning one of 'Blaudett's Cathedral Pastilles', so that there is now a smell of incense in the shop. On the wall a 'gold-framed toilet-water advertisement' displays a lady 'whose charms were unholily heightened by the glare from the red bottle in the window'; and it is evident that this 'flamboyant thing' constitutes a shrine to Mr. Shaynor. The narrator (apparently an established customer, who is very much at home) concocts for Shaynor an alcoholic drink compounded at random from the chemist's stock. Soon:

> Shaynor rose to his feet, his eyes fixed once more on the advertisement, where the young woman bathed in the light from the red jar simpered pinkly over her pearls. His lips moved without cessation. I stepped nearer to listen. 'And threw—and threw—and threw,' he repeated, his face all sharp with some inexplicable agony.
>
> I moved forward astonished. But it was then he found words—delivered roundly and clearly. These:
>
> 'And threw warm gules on Madeleine's young breast.'
>
> The trouble passed off his countenance, and he returned lightly to his place, rubbing his hands.

There is nothing particularly surprising in a young man's recalling, at a suitable prompting, and not quite accurately, a very famous line from Keats. But then Shaynor sits down and begins to write:

> I shut the door into the inner office and moved up behind him. He made no sign that he saw or heard. I looked over his shoulder, and read, amid half-formed words, sentences, and wild scratches:
>
> ——Very cold it was. Very cold
> The hare—the hare—the hare—
> The birds——

He raised his head sharply, and frowned toward the blank shutters of the poulterer's shop where they jutted out against our window. Then one clear line came:

The hare, in spite of fur, was very cold.

For some time we continue, by way of Shaynor's scribbling and murmuring, in this sort of struggling contact with the mind of a young man who died in 1821:

A fairyland for you and me
Across the foam—beyond . . .
A magic foam, a perilous sea.

Our windows fronting on the dangerous foam. . . .

Our open casements facing desolate seas
Forlorn—forlorn——

At length, after a moment of seeming agony, Shaynor stretches, yawns, and declares that he has had 'a bit of a doze'. The narrator asks him if he has ever read 'anything written by a man called Keats'. Shaynor says that he has not so much as heard the name. When told that Keats is 'rather what's called the lover's poet', he says: 'Indeed. I must dip into him.' But this, although he is ignorant of the fact, is just what Shaynor has been doing.

A great part of the effect of 'Wireless' comes from a very special use which Kipling here makes of the 'frame'. There is somebody else in the chemist's shop, besides Shaynor and the narrator. There is a Mr. Cashell, a nephew of the proprietor, and he comes bobbing in and out of a back room where he has installed a 'Marconi' machine for the transmission and reception of messages by the recently invented method of wireless telegraphy. He is waiting for a message from another amateur in the neighbouring seaside town of Poole, and meanwhile he displays his apparatus to the narrator:

'That's all,' he said, proudly, as though himself responsible for the wonder. 'That is the thing that will reveal to us the Powers—whatever the Powers may be—at work—through space—a long distance away. . . . We've all the night before us to see wonders.'

But there is a technical hitch, it seems, at the other end. Shaynor has just gone on from 'The hare, in spite of fur, was very cold' to something about incense and a darling picture framed in gold, when Mr. Cashell sticks his head in again. 'There's something coming through from somewhere,' he says. 'But it isn't Poole.'

There is another—and deeper—story of the supernatural in *Traffics and Discoveries:* 'They.' Here we start with a narrator who is very much taken up with, and pleased by, his motor-car—as we know Kipling to have been. Motor-cars are still a novelty, and it is an adventure to drive one sixty miles across the south of England. Amusing himself idly in this way, the narrator gets lost, and stumbles upon a country house and gardens of the most mellow beauty, owned by a blind maiden lady. The place is full of the voices and laughter of children; he glimpses a little girl at a high window; but throughout the story the children are elusive. It is evident that they make the blind woman's whole life. She asks the narrator if he is fond of children, and he gives her 'one or two reasons' why he does 'not altogether hate them'. They discuss dreams and the difficulty of seeing faces in dreams. 'I have never seen the faces of my dead in any dream,' he says.

The house, accepting another day at end, as it had accepted an hundred thousand gone, seemed to settle deeper into its rest among the shadows.

'Have you ever wanted to?' she said after the silence.

'Very much sometimes,' I replied.

We learn nothing more about the personal life of the narrator, although he makes two further visits to the beautiful house. Or we learn nothing more until almost the close of the story—and then full knowledge comes to us in a manner strangely oblique and moving. He is much drawn to the children, but none of them has ever spoken to him or touched him. A moment comes when some of them appear to be hiding gaily behind an old leather screen. The narrator taps on the screen, hoping to coax them out. But the lady is conducting business with a tenant who is demanding a new shed, and the narrator's attention strays to this. Then:

> I ceased to tap the leather—was, indeed, calculating the cost of the shed—when I felt my relaxed hand taken and turned softly between the soft hands of a child. So at last I had triumphed. In a moment I would turn and acquaint myself with those quick-footed wanderers. . . .
>
> The little brushing kiss fell in the centre of my palm—as a gift on which the fingers were, once, expected to close: as the all-faithful, half-reproachful signal of a waiting child not used to neglect even when grown-ups were busiest—a fragment of the mute code devised very long ago.
>
> Then I knew. And it was as though I had known from the first day when I looked across the lawn at the high window.

Beyond this, everything is left to us. We have to conclude that the children are not living children, and that the yearning love of the blind woman has drawn them from across the grave to this beautiful earthly place. It is the narrator's dead child who has kissed his hand. At the close of the story he recognizes that, however it may be with the blind woman, for him it would be wrong to accept this strange reunion. He goes away, and we are left with the certainty that he never drives up in his motor-car again.

We can readily see that the writing of 'They' must be connected with Kipling's memories of Josephine, who died in New York. Lockwood Kipling has a passage in a letter that bears on this: 'The house and garden are full of the lost child and poor Rud told his mother how he saw her when a door opened, when a space was vacant at table, coming out of every green dark corner of the garden.' The letter, written some years before 'They', might be a biographical gloss on the story. And there is a further point of biographical significance. Kipling's sister, Trix, who was subject to attacks of mental instability, is described by Mr. Carrington as ' "psychic", so unworldly that she seemed sometimes to move in a land of phantoms', and as 'hardly able to live a normal life'. But we know something more specific about Trix's 'psychic' side. She practised automatic writing, the technique whereby a medium, when in a trance, purports to transmit messages from the dead to the living. Trix, in fact, was 'Mrs. Holland', and it was 'A Report on Mrs. Holland's Script', printed in the *Proceedings* of the Society for Psychical Research, that prompted another English lady of unimpeachable character, Mrs. Coombe Tennant, to become, as 'Mrs. Willett', the most celebrated of all English mediums of this sort.

There is general agreement among critics that the greatest of Kipling's powers is his intuitive penetration into primitive states of consciousness in which reason merges with magic. He must have understood his sister's temperament very well, and indeed in some degree shared it. In 'They' he is giving imaginative form to a refusal to attempt communication with the dead. The best comment on the story is to be found, not in the rather sentimental poem ('The Return of the Children') with which it is prefaced, but in another and much sterner poem, 'Endor':

The road to En-dor is easy to tread
  For Mother or yearning Wife.
There, it is sure, we shall meet our Dead
  As they were even in life.
Earth has not dreamed of the blessing in store
For desolate hearts on the road to En-dor.

Whispers shall comfort us out of the dark—
  Hands—ah God!—that we knew!
Visions and voices—look and hark!—
  Shall prove that the tale is true,
And that those who have passed to the farther shore
May be hailed—at a price—on the road to En-dor . . .

Oh the road to En-dor is the oldest road
  And the craziest road of all!
Straight it runs to the Witch's abode,
  As it did in the days of Saul,
And nothing has changed of the sorrow in store
For such as go down on the road to En-dor!

In the biographical context which we have just been considering, this poem is a stiff warning to have constructed out of *I Samuel, xxviii*, 7. The portrait of a lady in 'They', on the other hand, reveals a new facet when we see its tender and delicate fantasy in that same context.

A very much later story, 'The Wish House' (*Debits and Credits*, 1926), may be mentioned here, although it is far too complex and subtle a creation for brief discussion. It tells how Mrs. Ashcroft, a cook, has practised a strange form of magic. If you can find a house which has stood long untenanted, and if it has a letter-box, then through this letter-box you can communicate with a Token—and this may be made the means of taking upon yourself disease or suffering being experienced by another.* Mrs. Ashcroft has done this, and now the wound she has thus accepted from a former lover has turned malignant, and she is dying. The strength of 'The Wish House' is in its grasp, in so humble and obscure a setting, of some of the high places of tragedy. Kipling's best critic, Dr. Tompkins, describes Mrs. Ashcroft as 'like a woman in the sagas, with much the same range of sensibility, the same ancient acceptance of the dark forces of life, and the same stark courage and laconic speech'. This is well said. In the sense that it is unmeaning to call Piero della Francesco's 'Resurrection' the world's greatest painting it is no doubt unmeaning to call 'The Wish House' its greatest short story. But it is at least one of the achievements which most certainly sets Kipling beside Guy de Maupassant and Anton Chekhov as a supreme master of the kind. It is a position which no other English-born writer has remotely approached.

* Kipling may have drawn the basis of this story from Indian legend. Edward Thompson (*A History of India*, 1927) records that the Emperor Babur was believed to have died vicariously for his son Humayun, who was ill with fever: 'Babur walked thrice round his bed, praying aloud, "On me be all that thou art suffering". He then cried, "I have prevailed! I have taken it!" and then went out to his own death-bed.' But belief in the possibility of thus accepting another's suffering has been widespread, and educated people are to be found who subscribe to it today.

CHAPTER EIGHT

FROM *THE JUNGLE BOOKS* TO *REWARDS AND FAIRIES*

THE JUNGLE BOOKS (1894–1895) were written in Vermont, and initiate a phase of Kipling's career in which he can be considered as having become a writer for children. On a superficial view, one might regard this development as being the consequence of some failure of confidence in himself as a 'serious' author. He certainly did not so estimate the situation. Writing retrospectively in *Something of Myself*, he has more to say about the group of children's books than about any other—and indeed it is his main point that only in a limited sense ought they to be regarded as children's books at all. Most mature readers who like Kipling will be found to agree with him in this. And the books are most keenly appreciated by those who read them first in childhood (or listened to them being read) and have then come back to them in later life. This is the road to finding those layers of significance which Kipling, in fact, claimed to have put into them.

A child's natural start is with *Just So Stories* (1902), which is above everything else a nursery book. Nothing in English is more unchallengeably the work of one who possessed the art of telling stories to children, and who enjoyed exercising it. The narrative style, seemingly so naïve and spontaneous, represents in fact one of the most notable triumphs of Kipling's craft. And here he had to overcome a bad or unreflecting habit which he had caught from the taste of the age: that of introducing into writing for or about children a sentimental convention of baby-talk. In the *Just So Stories* the element of misapplied, invented and oddly transformed words renders a wholly different effect. It is felt from the start as part of the ritual of a special or secret language which the narrator shares with his hearers, and it is associated with infancy only in the sense of wonderfully suggesting the infancy of the world, when all creatures and things were pristine and plastic still. The style is, moreover, and in a degree varying from story to story and from place to place within a story, incantatory and therefore full of a strong magic; and it is capable (as in 'The Sing-Song of Old Man Kangaroo') of compassing rhythmical effects which are totally new.

The *Just So Stories* are often compared with Lewis Carroll's *Alice's Adventures in Wonderland* and *Through the Looking Glass* as the greatest English achievements in writing for young children. Carroll shares with Kipling the faculty of appealing to children and adults alike. With each there is a certain hit-or-miss element to be observed, since there are some children and adults upon whom the magic of one, or both, fails to work. Each inhabits what must be called a real world, although it is certainly not an actual world. Carroll's is the world of dream, although of dream at once drastically censored and cunningly intellectualized in the interest of a rather egg-headed Oxford nursery. Kipling's is the world of myth.

Most of the *Just So Stories*, indeed, are myths of the kind known as *aetiological*. An aetiological myth is one evolved—generally in a more or less 'primitive' society—to explain and render intelligible some existing state of affairs which in itself perplexes and challenges the human spirit. The most famous of all aetiological myths is that of the Creation and Fall of Man as it is recounted in the Book of Genesis. In this, answers to nearly all the great riddles are bound together within a single narrative satisfying to the imagination—and satisfying, too, to the intellect working within the limits of a 'pre-scientific' cultural context. The *Just So Stories* are little myths solving little riddles: how the camel got anything so strange as a hump, and the elephant anything so strange as a trunk. It is true that, to be quite accurate, we must qualify the description of these stories as myths. They have been invented for the satisfaction not of a primitive people but of modern children, who are 'primitive' only in the metaphorical sense that their intellectual development does, to some extent, recapitulate the course of human evolution. This is why the stories are made to hover—and, again, it is a miracle of craft—between a level of fantasy and a level of simple conviction. So in one aspect they are like make-believe games, such as children love. In another, they are an introduction to one of the great literary kinds—a kind reflecting something radical in the development of the human imagination. To appreciate *Just So Stories* is to establish a basis for appreciating *Paradise Lost* or *Moby Dick*.

The fame of *The Jungle Book* and *The Second Jungle Book*—the most widely popular of all Kipling's writings—is owing to their central figure, Mowgli, the child nurtured by wolves, who survives and grows to manhood as Master of the Jungle. Mowgli's origin (as a literary creation, that is) is attended by some obscurity, and it is best to begin with the last that we hear about him. This is in 'In the Rukh' (*Many Inventions*), a story designed to be entirely realistic, and quite certainly not written for young readers. Gisborne, an officer of the Indian Department of Woods and Forests, encounters on the fringes of the jungle a beautiful youth, 'naked except for the loin-cloth, but crowned with a wreath of the tasselled blossoms of the white convolvulus creeper', and with a voice 'clear and bell-like, utterly different from the usual whine of the native'. He is like an angel, we are told—or, better, like a Greek god: one of 'the illustrations in the Classical Dictionary', as Gisborne puts it to himself. His name is Mowgli, and he proves to have an amazing command over all the animals of the *rukh*. He takes service with Gisborne; and later Gisborne's superior, a German named Muller who has immense experience of the ways of the jungle, understands his case:

> 'I tell you dot only once in my service, and dot is thirty years, haf I met a boy dot began as this man began. Und he died. Sometimes you hear of dem in der census reports, but dey all die. Dis man haf lived, and he is an anachronism, for he is before der Iron Age, and der Stone Age. Look here, he is at der beginnings of der history of man—Adam in der Garden, und now we want only an Eva!'

Mowgli gains an Eva, in the person of the ill-treated daughter of Gisborne's native butler: it is the speed with which he not only woos her but wins her that makes it certain that Kipling was not writing for children here. We overhear Mowgli's explaining himself to his bride. Reared by wolves and with wolf-cubs as his foster brothers, he had grown up among the beasts until a time came when the beasts told him to go. He had then become a herder of cattle among men, but had been driven out by them when the old woman who looked after him had seen him playing with his 'brethren' by night. Since then he had been a wanderer—but now as an employee of the

Department of Woods and Forests he will receive a wage and a pension. At the end of the story we have glimpse of Mowgli's first child, guarded by a wolf.

What is interesting about 'In the Rukh' is the entire absence of the magic which the *Jungle Books* were going to create. Kipling has not yet glimpsed what material he has under his hand; this Mowgli is an implausible mixture of Noble Savage, Indian native properly respectful of the *raj*, and a godling strayed out of Greek mythology in a manner rather reminiscent of some of the more whimsical short stories of E. M. Forster. Mowgli plays a flute, 'as it might have been the song of some wandering wood-god'. This last association is emphasized; 'the hint of the wood-god was not to be mistaken', we are told a few pages later.

'In the Rukh' was almost certainly written before Kipling had conceived the Mowgli stories proper, but in its published form it may embody revisions designed to make it fit in with the evolving series. As it is, Mowgli's story seems to have been developed without much planning. Taking the two *Jungle Books* together, he appears in eight out of fifteen stories—including the first, which begins with his being adopted by wolf parents, and the last, which tells of his final departure from the world of the beasts. That there is true imaginative coherence between the Mowgli stories proper appears as soon as we try to set this last of them, 'The Spring Running', in any relationship with 'In the Rukh'. The Mowgli of 'In the Rukh' walks into the story with nothing much behind him except (with an obvious effect of paradox) certain unusual educational advantages. 'Hard exercise, the best of good eating, and baths whenever he felt in the least hot or dusty, had given him strength and growth far beyond his age.' He is a cross between a Wordsworthian child of nature and a Boy Scout. He walks out of the story at the other end in the company of a nice girl and with the intention of settling down. He knows all the answers—just as the uninspired Kipling always did. The Mowgli of 'The Spring Running', on the contrary, knows neither his world nor himself with any certainty, because he is a human spirit in the throes of some painful and mysterious process of growth. It is spring. 'The year turns,' Bagheera the Black Panther tells him. 'The Jungle goes forward. The Time of New Talk is near.' Mowgli must have heard this before. But now he is on the verge of manhood, and there faces him a hard truth, obscurely seen. A boy may run with the Jungle People, but 'Man goes to Man'. His old companions do not reject him, but—*this* spring, he notices it—they come tardily at his summons, having concerns which can be none of his. Yet all this, and the mere surface solution of his problem in the last pages of the story, make too finite and identifiable the occasion of the unhappiness that has come to Mowgli. Something else is elusively present.

This is a characteristic of all the Mowgli stories. All are moral fables—even to the extent of sometimes making us feel that Mowgli is over-lavishly provided with tutors, and is rather constantly having to put up with what the hymn calls Instruction's warning Voice. But this is not, in fact, oppressive—perhaps because there is always some hinted further significance which we have to strain to catch. Take, for example, the monkey-folk, the *Bandar-log*. They stand for something outside themselves, answer to something in our own experience which we are not proud of. But just what? Here, and in some other places, the fable beckons us to territory where we must think for ourselves. And there is one puzzle bigger than all the others. It is what the books mean when they talk about the Law.

In the *Second Jungle Book* there is a poem called 'The Law of the Jungle'. A schoolmaster might call this title an oxymoron —'a rhetorical figure by which contradictory terms are conjoined'. For the jungle is, almost by definition, lawless; we call this, that or the other human activity a 'jungle' when we are thinking of some area of savage competition in which no holds are barred. But Kipling's poem turns out to be a set of rules for wolves. Some of them are again of the boy-scout order: 'Wash daily from nose-tip to tail-tip.' But in general they provide a sensible code for conducting the necessarily predatory and lethal routine of a wolf pack on lines which will preserve the pack's social cohesion—and also in terms of what we must think of as fair play. This conception will not impress us in itself. Children, who feel no impassable gulf between the animal world and the nursery, expect the idea of 'what is fair' to obtain in the one as in the other; and they are reassured when they find it so represented to them. Hence hosts of juvenile beast-fables designed for edification. Kipling designs edification, and in this interest contrives to give his Law almost crushing force:

Now these are the Laws of the Jungle, and many and
mighty are they;
But the head and the hoof of the Law and the haunch
and the hump is—Obey!

If we wish to criticize the whole conception we shall probably say that, here in the context of the *Jungle Books*, Kipling is casting the impressive disguise of authentic moral law over certain aspects of animal behaviour instinctively evolved to secure the survival of a species. To test the validity of this criticism we should have to enter deeply into Kipling's theory of society. He certainly believed that moral ideas can be derived only from experience, but that as there is much that is common and universal in all human experience so is there a common and universal Law lying beneath all the variations of racial and national cultures. It is a Law codified in custom, and its recognition and preservation is the distinguishing principle of Civilization. Peoples or societies or individuals ignoring the Law thereby diminish themselves—becoming (in the famous and unfortunately ambiguous phrase in 'Recessional') 'lesser breeds'. To show a wolf pack as within the Law, and a chatter of monkeys as outside it, is simply to use the method of fable to enforce the depth and reach of the idea. But to account for the appeal of the *Jungle Books* we have to go back to Kipling's almost unexampled command of the sense of wonder; his power to bring, as from very far away, reports which validate themselves in the telling, so that our disbelief is suspended in the face of whole new ranges of experience.

Kim, published in 1901, comes at about the mid-point of the phase of Kipling's writing which we are considering. Many regard it as his masterpiece, and there was nothing which gave him more trouble—before which, that is to say, he found more difficulty in satisfying himself. The book appears to have grown, in some degree, out of *Mother Maturin*, the abortive and obviously immature novel about which we hear a good deal during his early career as a writer. He more than once got 'stuck' with *Kim*, and had to turn to other things. More, perhaps, than any other of his productions, it required 'smoking' by his father. This was partly because Lockwood Kipling knew far more about India than did even his son, and had a present and not merely retrospective command of it. But, more essentially, it was because this had to be, of all his books, the one most his father's book in temper and vision. It comes, in fact, from that level of his experience when he was first learning to see through his father's eyes, and feel in his father's fashion. What is evoked is the India of the child Kipling, not of the young man.

Today it is only here and there that one finds an educated Indian to speak any good of Kipling, for to most he is simply the celebrant, in poetry and prose, of an alien rule now overthrown. It is almost possible to feel that, had he published only *Kim*, it might have been different. At least to a Western reader, it is the Indian characters in the story who appear most real and, in a deep sense, most beloved. (Indeed, there is a further truth here: one which it takes a poet's sensitiveness to discern. Throughout the Indian tales, T. S. Eliot says, 'it is on the whole the Indian characters who have the greater reality, because they are treated with the understanding of love'.)

Kim himself, the lower-class Anglo-Indian waif growing up in the native bazaars, clearly owns some descent from Mowgli, who grew up in the jungle. And Kim's lama, whom Kim comes to serve faithfully, and who in turn risks forfeiting his life's goal to go to the help of the boy—Kim's lama, too, has an ancestor in the *Jungle Books*. In 'The Miracle of Purun Bhagat' there are no *Bandar-log*, and the *langurs*, 'the big gray-whiskered monkeys of the Himalayas,' may share the blanket of a saint, since to holiness all things are holy. This story has a purity and limpidity such as Kipling seldom achieves, but which is carried over into the relevant parts of *Kim*. Kim's lama is not merely a product of obervation and a whimsical sympathy. Behind him is his creator's sense that beyond the *pax Britannica*, and having nothing to do with it, there lies, perhaps, a peace passing understanding; and that it is not his own people who have evolved the form of religious consciousness most attuned to it.

These are strange terms in which to consider a boy's story, a 'Secret Service' romance. But *Kim* is not a simple book, and even mature critics may be deceived by it. Mr. Edmund Wilson believes that Kipling got it wrong—and got it wrong because he was not intelligent enough to get it right. Our expectation is betrayed, Mr. Wilson asserts. The theme is (or should be) the gradual dawning of Kim's consciousness that he is really a *sahib*. 'What the reader tends to expect is that Kim will come eventually to realize that he is delivering into bondage to the British invaders those whom he has always considered his own people, and that a struggle between allegiances will result.' This is quite wrong. Nothing in the book conjures up such an expectation. It is true that Kim becomes conscious of being a *sahib*, and true that this confronts him with a divided loyalty. But it is a loyalty divided between two ways of life, not two political allegiances. On the one hand is a secular life, the duties of which—if in a boy's terms—Kim understands well. It is the task of the courageous, the resourceful and the bold to guard the frontier, to hold the wall. On the other hand there is the life of contemplation, which Kim can just glimpse through the lama's eyes. But this divided loyalty scarcely means that Kim has to make a choice. That choice has been made for him by the whole structure of the society in which he has been brought up. It is his destiny to play the Great Game. Cunning may enable him to obtain, within the rules of the Game, a role in which he can serve and protect his lama still. But he is a servant and protector, not a disciple. 'It is too high for me', he says, when his master has preached his most impressive sermon. Still, Kim's imagination and intellect have been touched by the knowledge that there is another Way than the way of armies and cleverly disguised policemen. He is taken no further than that. Once more, something is left to us, should we care to think about it.

In *Puck of Pook's Hill* (1906) and *Rewards and Fairies* (1910) two English children, a boy and a girl, have a series of magical encounters, round and about their father's estate, with people of many races—British, Pictish, Roman, Saxon, Norman, Jewish—whose stories are woven into the continuing texture of English history. These are books for children in so far as nothing is admitted to them that is unfit for the knowledge and attention of children. But it is by omission rather than by distortion that this propriety is achieved. They are books for mature readers because Kipling has written into them—always by means of imaginative implication rather than explicit statement—convictions to which his own mature faith is given. It is a faith that a nation and a civilization, once painfully forged, will survive only through as many generations as are prepared to meet new conditions and new challenges armed with all the strength and wisdom that tradition and custom provide.

That there is a lesson in our history-lessons is an idea as old as Dionysius of Halicarnassus, who said that History is Philosophy teaching by examples. Not all modern historians would agree that the lesson is easy to identify, and plenty of mediocre books have been written in which a pageant of history has been unfolded by writers having moral designs upon young people. What raises the *Puck* stories immeasurably above these is, once more, the power of Kipling's historical imagination, and the reach and certainty of his art wherever essentials are in question. Of his sureness of touch we have an example in the way the magic is made to work. Dan and Una are a little surprised and awed by the company which Puck—often quite unobtrusively—summons up for them. But not much is made of this; nor, answeringly, of the bewilderment which the visitors feel when aware of a superficially changed environment. And 'visitors' seems the right term to employ. Sir Richard Dalyngridge and Parnesius, Hal o' the Draft and Kadmiel, Nicholas Culpeper and the rest have no sense of themselves as ghosts or apparitions; they come and go with no more than a hint of magic, taking the same pleasure in the children's society as the children take in theirs. Parnesius, the young Roman centurion, is naturally interested in Dan's catapult; the elastic takes him by surprise so that he hits himself squarely on the nail—and then in no time he is describing his family (who have lived in Britain for generations), and how as a child he used to be taken for holidays to Aquae Sulis (which is the English town of Bath):

> 'The best baths in Britain. Just as good, I'm told, as Rome. All the old gluttons sit in hot water, and talk scandal and politics. And the Generals come through the streets with their guards behind them; and the magistrates come in their chairs with their stiff guards behind them; and you meet fortune-tellers, and goldsmiths, and merchants, and philosophers, and feather-sellers, and ultra-Roman Britons, and ultra-British Romans, and tame tribesmen pretending to be civilized, and Jew lecturers, and—oh, everybody interesting.'

We may think to catch an echo from some modern Indian city, with its august English officials and its crowded bazaars, in this description. Indeed, it is sometimes said that Parnesius and his friend Pertinax, who guard Hadrian's Wall against the Picts and the Winged Hats, are a little too like officers of the Indian Army, similarly standing guard on the North-West Frontier. It has been pointed out, too, that there is significance in Kipling's setting this group of stories in the period of the decay of Roman power in Britain, since the break-up of the British Empire was already haunting his mind. But these similitudes are not made to intrude upon us, and they are very far from impairing the illusion. There is no reason to suppose that Roman Britain had obtained any early hold on Kipling's imagination. But we are likely to have an uncanny sense as we read that the author simply *must* have been there; have seen with his own eyes what he now describes to us. *Kim* itself carries no greater impression of authenticity. This extraordinary power can best be illustrated by a single quotation of some length. Parnesius is marching North for the first time, in command of reinforcements for the garrison of the Wall. And even on this side of the frontier there are signs that a great Roman province is already in decline:

> 'Of course, the farther North you go the emptier are the roads. At last you fetch clear of the forests and climb bare hills, where wolves howl in the ruins of our cities that have been. No more pretty girls; no more jolly magistrates who knew your Father when he was young, and invite you to stay with them; no news at the temples and way-stations except bad news of wild beasts. There's where you meet hunters, and trappers for the Circuses, prodding along chained bears and muzzled wolves. Your pony shies at them, and your men laugh.
>
> 'The houses change from gardened villas to shut forts with watch-towers of grey stone, and great stone-walled sheep-folds, guarded by armed Britons of the North Shore. In the naked hills beyond the naked houses, where the shadows of the clouds play like cavalry charging, you see puffs of black smoke from the mines. The hard road goes on and on—and the wind sings through your helmet-plume—past altars to Legions and Generals forgotten, and broken statues of Gods and Heroes, and thousands of graves where the mountain foxes and hares peep at you. Red-hot in summer, freezing

in winter, is that big, purple heather country of broken stone.

'Just when you think you are at the world's end, you see a smoke from East to West as far as the eye can turn, and then, under it, also as far as the eye can stretch, houses and temples, shops and theatres, barracks and granaries, trickling along like dice behind—always behind—one long, low, rising and falling, and hiding and showing line of towers. And that is the Wall!'

Some of the stories take Kipling's imagination farther afield than Hadrian's Wall, or even the lost province of Velentia which lay beyond it. But in *Something of Myself* he makes very clear the extent to which he regarded the whole series as home-based; based, that is to say, upon all that could be seen, and much that could be excavated, on the small estate in Sussex which was his eventual home. His own children had been given a birch-bark canoe; they had acted scenes from *A Midsummer Night's Dream* in their own meadow; a few fields away lay 'an old and unshifting Fairy Ring', and so did 'the long, overgrown slag-heap of a most ancient forge, supposed to have been worked by the Phoenicians and Romans, and, since then, uninterruptedly till the middle of the eighteenth century'. The digging of a well yielded 'a Jacobean tobacco-pipe, a worn Cromwellian latten spoon and, at the bottom of all, the bronze cheek of a Roman horse-bit', and the cleaning out of an old pond produced two Elizabethan 'sealed quarts' and 'a perfectly polished Neolithic axe-head'.

Kipling had lived in his Sussex home for thirty years when he called up and recorded these memories, and the emphasis which he places upon them as a source of inspiration somehow sets us wondering. T. S. Eliot, in an essay to which we shall return, speaks of him as having 'a peculiar detachment and remoteness from all environment . . . a remoteness as of an alarmingly intelligent visitor from another planet'. It is certainly true that Kipling put his roots down late, and that the attachment to Sussex which the *Puck* stories celebrate has about it some hint of a resolute act of the will. Set at the entrance to *Rewards and Fairies* is a poem, 'A Charm', beginning:

Take of English earth as much
As either hand may rightly clutch . . .

'Lay that earth upon thy heart', it goes on, and continues:

It shall sweeten and make whole
Fevered breath and festered soul;
It shall mightily restrain
Over-busy hand and brain;
It shall ease thy mortal strife
'Gainst the immortal woe of life,
Till thyself restored shall prove
By what grace the Heavens do move.

This is as near any private prayer of his own as Kipling admits us to.

CHAPTER NINE

STALKY AND OTHERS

IT WAS SHORTLY after giving up his home in Vermont that Kipling started to write his school-stories, and it is possible to view these, like the work considered in the preceding chapter, as the harking back into pre-adult experience of a mind in some way held up in its natural progress towards fully matured accomplishment. But if the Stalky stories concern adolescence and make their greatest appeal to adolescents, Kipling appears to have regarded them as addressed as much to educators as to those suffering education. 'There came to me,' he records, 'the idea of beginning some tracts or parables on the education of the young. These, for reasons honestly beyond my control, turned themselves into a series of tales called *Stalky & Co.*' And then, as if he feels that he has allowed too much to this involuntary element of transformation, he adds of the book: 'It is still read [he is writing in 1935] and I maintain it is a truly valuable collection of tracts.'

School-stories (like animal stories) that were substantially 'tracts'—having massive moral designs on young readers—were common enough in the later nineteenth century. The most famous of all such stories, Thomas Hughes's *Tom Brown's School-days*, is in some aspects a firmly realistic picture of life at Rugby under the headmastership of Thomas Arnold, and it contains episodes of schoolboy brutality which exceed anything Kipling was to produce; its main purpose, however, was to display Arnold as an inspired educator of Christian gentlemen. And Hughes's Christians are of the 'muscular' sort admired by his friends F. D. Maurice and Charles Kingsley; he had himself written a book entitled *The Manliness of Christ.* Two other famous school-stories of the age—*Eric, or Little by Little*, and *St. Winifred's, or The World of School*—were the work of a clergyman, Dean Farrar, who took the very darkest view of a schoolboy's chances of salvation. Kipling's heroes have 'an intimate and unholy acquaintance' with *Eric* and *St. Winifred's;* they rejoice, that is to say, in Farrar's books as objects of ridicule. 'Didn't I "Eric" 'em splendidly?' Beetle asks, after having treated the Sixth Formers to a burlesque of a master's moralizing; and on another occasion he says: 'We ain't goin' to have any beastly Erickin'.' Kipling was always to be dead against all preaching at schoolboys; of Westward Ho! he records with satisfaction:

> Except in the case of two House-masters I do not recall being lectured or preached at on morals or virtue. It is not always expedient to excite a growing youth's religious emotions, because one set of nerves seems to communicate with others, and Heaven knows what mines a 'pi-jaw' may touch off.

This is a penetrating remark, and there can be no doubt that Kipling felt both that he had serious things to say on education, and that if they were to be said through his own medium—which was fiction—the doctrinal intent must be cunningly disguised. Hence the dominant surface effect of the Stalky stories: that of gloriously boisterous young rebels, ceaselessly engaged in harrying authority as embodied in their masters and prefects; gloating when they succeed ('I gloat, I gloat!' is their accepted paean of triumph); and taking their lines or lickings nonchalantly when they fail. But it is only in one or two of the stories that Kipling may be said to have been carried away into celebrating this turbulence for its own sake. They are all, indeed, wildly exaggerated pictures of school life, much closer to the fantasies of boyhood than to actual boyhood experience. But with this (which owes a little to Dickens and a good deal to Mark Twain) there is blended an undoubted seriousness of intent. This is what makes *Stalky & Co.* a book quite as much for adults as adolescents. Kipling is saying something—and something over which his readers may disagree violently. Right from the beginning, indeed, it was a controversial book.

Let us start with the most controversial story of all: 'The Moral Reformers'. Sefton and Campbell are among the biggest boys in the school, and a hint from the chaplain reveals to Stalky, M'Turk and Beetle that they have been bullying a small boy so cruelly that he has been reduced to dumb misery—just as Beetle (who is Kipling) was in his first term:

> 'But I got it worse than any one,' said Beetle. 'If you want an

authority on bullyin', Padre, come to me. Corkscrews — brush-drill — keys — head-knucklin' — arm-twistin' — rockin'—Ag Ags—and all the rest of it.'

The bullies are too strong to be tackled head on. So Stalky and Co. adopt a stratagem which results in their being able to tie up their victims helplessly—and then, over many pages of the story, they put them through all the tortures (which seems to be the proper word) that Beetle remembers. 'Corkscrews' has nothing to do with opening bottles; 'brush-drill' doesn't need a brush, nor 'keys' a key. This long passage is a masterpiece of sinister reticences. Sefton and Campbell are only released when they have been so much hurt that they are likely to remain broken and abject for keeps. Even so, and when the three executioners are all 'dripping with excitement and exertion', there is a moment when Beetle wants to go on. 'I've had it done to me,' he says, and when he has been stopped, Stalky's verdict is: 'This moral suasion biznai takes it out of a chap.'

Not surprisingly, 'The Moral Reformers' has horrified a good many people—including H. G. Wells, who viewed it as an involuntary give-away of the hideous wickedness of the British Empire. We need not take so extreme a view. Kipling is here trying to write, as he always tries to write, of 'things as they are'. Violence breeds violence, and cruelty suffered leads to cruelty inflicted. Early in the story, Beetle shows himself quite clear-headed about bullying. 'Bullies like bullyin',' he says. 'They mean it. They think it up in lesson and practise it in the quarters.' At the end he just stops himself from thus bullying for the sheer sake of bullying. All moral reformers, we may suppose, are at some moral hazard. The very title of the story carries a muted irony.

The first-written of the stories, 'Slaves of the Lamp', is in two parts. In the first the boys are rehearsing a school pantomime, and make so much noise that they incur the wrath of Mr. King, a house-master who, although an able teacher, is represented as never addressing his pupils except with a fluent and stinging sarcasm. (Beetle, although his sworn enemy, is a close student of King's superb rhetorical performances, since Beetle is himself resolved to be a lord of language. We ought always to study, and learn from, our opponents.) The boys swear revenge—but it has to be revenge in terms of that maxim of Stalky's which marks him out as a great tactician: 'Not the least good having a row with a master unless you can make an ass of him'—and without his even knowing that it is you who have done it. Stalky ingeniously engineers a flare-up of temper between King and Rabbits-Eggs—which is the name the school has given to the local carrier, a rustic character of primitive intelligence and violent instinct. Rabbits-Eggs hurls stones at King in his study window so accurately and pertinaciously that the room is presently a shambles—partly because, in the confusion, Beetle furthers the good work by scattering ink and (apparently) scarring with a flint the spines of King's particularly handsome set of Gibbon's *Decline and Fall of the Roman Empire*. Moreover, Manders minor, who had offended Stalky & Co., is found to be 'bleeding profusely from a cut on the cheekbone', so that, as well as ink and gum, there is 'blood on the books and papers'. This is a most satisfactory affair. 'Everybody paid in full—beautiful feelin' ', is M'Turk's verdict on it.

The second part of 'Slaves of the Lamp' is set among a gathering of Old Boys of the school several years later. They learn how Stalky, as an officer fighting on the North-West frontier of India, gets his troops out of a trap by ingeniously exploiting the enmity between two of the hostile tribes, so that they turn upon each other, with Stalky himself remaining invisible. Stalky has brought off his old trick again, and soldiers who might have been annihilated escape with minor casualties. Near the end of the story there is the following dialogue:

> 'I see,' said Dick Four, nodding. 'Practically he duplicated that trick over again. There's nobody like Stalky.'
>
> 'That's just where you make the mistake,' I said. 'India's full of Stalkies—Cheltenham and Haileybury and Marlborough chaps—that we don't know anything about, and the surprises will begin when there is really a big row on.'
>
> 'Who will be surprised?' said Dick Four.
>
> 'The other side. The gentlemen who go to the front in first-class carriages. Just imagine Stalky let loose on the south side of Europe with a sufficiency of Sikhs and a reasonable prospect of loot. Consider it quietly.'

Stalky never was to be so 'let loose'. But Indian soldiers were to fight in the British armies in Flanders in 1914, their first appearance on a European battlefield since Indian archers opposed the Greeks at Plataea in 479 B.C. (This is a useful reminder of the time-scale in terms of which it is necessary to consider Indian history.)

'Slaves of the Lamp' is an exuberant story, but it is not difficult to distinguish its serious aspect as a 'tract'. 'Blood on the books and papers.' E. M. Forster, who does not greatly care for Kipling, will be found to employ much the same symbolism in describing the fate of Lucy Honeychurch's photographs in *A Room with a View*. If we are to preserve the achievements of our civilization we must be prepared to fight for them. And we shall do this most effectively if we have been bred not too soft. That is what is happening at Westward Ho! In 'In Ambush', the first story in the book, we are told that the boys 'were learning, at the expense of a fellow-countryman, the lesson of their race, which is to put away all emotion and entrap the alien at the proper time'.

Equally important is something they are *not* learning, and which is trenchantly expressed in the story 'The Flag of their Country'. We have to remember that, more than any other school in England at the time, Westward Ho! was concentrating upon preparing boys to be officers in the British Army. Curiously enough (or so we may think, because it would be otherwise in such a school today), there was no military training whatever. Mr. Carrington puts this clearly:

> . . . the United Services College was an unlike a 'Military Academy' as a school could be. . . . There were no parades, no uniforms, no bands or flags, no school cadet corps, no patriotic propaganda, nor would it have occurred to any master or boy that such things could be regarded as anything but gross bad form.

In the story an elderly General who is on the governing Council of the school tries to insist that there *should* be a cadet corps. The Head clearly disapproves, but agrees that an experiment shall be made. The plan has a very poor reception from the boys, but eventually gets under way with some of them on the purely practical score that a knowledge of elementary drill will cut down the time they have to spend on this rather boring part of an officer's training when they go on to Sandhurst. So Foxy, the school's gym instructor (a retired N.C.O.), is given charge of the parades. These go tolerably well until a frightful thing happens. The General sends down a certain Mr. Martin (he is a Member of Parliament, which is something never to be much loved by Kipling), who harangues the boys about the time when they shall be 'leading their men against the bullets of England's foes . . . confronting the stricken field in all the pride of their youthful manhood'. The boys are staggered:

> Now the reserve of a boy is tenfold deeper than the reserve of a maid, she being made for one end only by blind Nature, but man for several. With a large and healthy hand, he tore down these veils, and trampled them under the well-intentioned feet of eloquence. In a raucous voice he cried aloud little matters, like the hope of Honour and the dream of Glory, that boys do not discuss even with their most intimate equals; cheerfully assuming that, till he spoke, they had never considered these possibilities. He pointed them to shining goals, with fingers which smudged out all radiance on all horizons. He profaned the most secret places of their souls with outcries and gesticulations.

All this is bad enough. But now Mr. Martin does an incredible thing. This, he says, is the concrete symbol of their land—and let no boy look on it who is not resolved to add to its imperishable lustre. By this time, Mr. Martin has produced, and is waving, 'a large calico Union Jack'. And he is waiting for the thunder of applause that should crown his effort:

> They looked in silence. They had certainly seen the thing before—down at the coastguard station, or through a telescope, half-mast high when a brig went ashore on Braunton sands; above the roof of the Golf Club, and in Keyte's window, where a certain kind of striped sweetmeat bore it in paper on each box. But the College never displayed it; it was no part of the scheme of their lives; the Head had never alluded to it; their fathers had not declared it unto them. It was a matter shut up, sacred and apart. What, in the name of everything caddish, was he driving at, who waved that horror before their eyes? Happy thought! Perhaps he was drunk.

Only Foxy, a man of the people, is touched and edified by Mr. Martin's flag-wagging. To gentlemen such pawing-over of sacred things is an unspeakable act.

We are not to suppose that Kipling himself regarded the Union Jack (more correctly to be called the Union Flag) as a *tabu* object. He would have approved the rhetoric of Thomas Campbell—

> The meteor flag of England
> Shall yet terrific burn—

and he himself could produce the same sort of thing, better done:

> Never the lotos closes, never the wild-fowl wake,
> But a soul goes out on the East Wind that died for
> England's sake—
> Man or woman or suckling, mother or bride or maid—
> Because on the bones of the English the English
> Flag is stayed.

It is simply that something about which one feels like that can readily be cheapened. Stalky, certainly, feels so degraded by the visitor's disastrous performance that—for the first and last time in his saga—he is discovered in tears. We feel that Kipling is putting all he has into this story. Some of the effects are a little broad; for example, we are several times told in a parenthesis that such or such a boy now suffering Mr. Martin's eloquence will within a few years be dead on one battlefield or another. But, all in all, it is perhaps 'The Flag of their Country', and not 'The Moral Reformers', which is the test case in *Stalky & Co.* Anybody who sees what this story is about will like the whole book.

In one of the best of the Indian Army stories, 'His Private Honour' (*Many Inventions*), Private Ortheris, who has a just score to settle with an officer who has struck him on parade (an offence for which the officer would be broken instantly were the incident to become officially known), pours scorn on the notion that he, Ortheris, being a man with a respect for his own manhood, should go to work by way of publicly claiming his 'rights'. In 'An Unsavoury Interlude' (a story disliked by many, since it exploits the worst that ruthless boys can achieve with a very dead cat) Stalky is expressing something of the same sort when he says to Beetle: 'My Hat! You've been here six years, and you expect fairness. Well, you *are* a dithering idiot.' It is a constant theme of *Stalky & Co.* that ours is a world in which we are lucky if even the roughest justice comes our way. The Head is represented as seldom caning a boy without trying to convince him that the punishment is, at least in some degree, arbitrary and unaccountable. He says: 'I'm going to execute you without rhyme, Beetle, or reason', or 'There's a certain flagrant injustice about this that ought to appeal to—your temperament'. (The break in this last speech is meant to mark a moment of impact.) Yet Stalky & Co., and all their companions, admire the Head enormously—quite as much as the real boys admired the real, and very much gentler, Cormell Price. Why does Kipling transform Price so strangely? The easy answer is that the inflicting of physical pain had a morbid attraction for Kipling, and that he exploits its being meted out as punishment to make it respectable. Some evidence can be brought forward to support this view; for example, in *Something of Myself* he tells us the result of his having heard of Dante's nine-ringed Hell:

> I bought a fat, American cloth-bound notebook, and set to work on an *Inferno*, into which I put, under appropriate torture, all my friends and most of the masters. This was really remunerative because one could chant his future doom to a victim walking below the windows of the study which I with my two companions now possessed.

But this confession fails, somehow, to come to us as particularly unwholesome. And if the 'Proosian Bates' disconcerts us, it is not because he is a sadist. It is because he has been made so concentrated a symbol of two ideas which might be better untelescoped. He stands (as does his school) both for the universe as a play of natural forces—unaccountable as a cyclone—and for the human wisdom which knows best how to temper us to take that universe's strain. And he certainly seems to believe that we are likely to put up a better show if we have been allowed in youth to behave in a fairly cyclonic way ourselves.

Kipling made several additions to the 'Stalky' saga quite

late in life. Two of these appear in the volume *Debits and Credits*. The first, 'The United Idolators', is a riotous story about a riot. *Uncle Remus* has swept the school. Somebody acquires a tortoise and paints it with King's House-colours; it becomes Brer Terrapin. Stalky & Co., of Prout's House, reply by fabricating a Tar Baby; and under these two totems tremendous battles take place. The resulting devastation, Mr. King says, is 'the natural corollary to dabbling in so-called transatlantic humour'. It is hard to dig any moral out of this engaging story. And so with 'The Propagation of Knowledge', in which Beetle, first to the gratification and then to the bewilderment of King, provides everybody with scraps of English literary history which they then pretend have come to them in the course of extensive reading; the story has a climax when the boys contrive that King shall be publicly commended by an External Examiner for advancing the view that Shakespeare's plays were written by Sir Francis Bacon—a piece of nonsense in the face of which King, in fact, always sees red. This is a very neat yarn, which carries no reverberation outside itself.

It is otherwise with 'Regulus', a story to be found in *A Diversity of Creatures* (1917). This is another test-case—and the present writer must put himself on record as having failed with it a number of years ago. He described it as 'surely puerile rather than vicious', and declared its subject to be 'the beating by the Captain of Games of a friend and study-mate who would have been exempt from this penalty had his First Fifteen Cap arrived in time from the school outfitter'. Second thoughts have convinced him that this is a misleading and inadequate account.

Kipling prefaces the story with a little Roman history:

> Regulus, a Roman general, defeated the Carthaginians 256 B.C., but was next year defeated and taken prisoner by the Carthaginians, who sent him to Rome with an embassy to ask for peace or an exchange of prisoners. Regulus strongly advised the Roman Senate to make no terms with the enemy. He then returned to Carthage and was put to death.

In point of fact, Regulus faced no simple death—and he knew it. In Kipling's story this only comes to us in the Latin lesson with which it starts (and which is given nearly in full). 'Now then,' Mr. King says, 'for *atqui sciebat quae sibi barbarus tortor pararet*'—and a boy called Winton addresses himself to the task of translation.

Winton is to be the central figure of the story: 'a long, heavy, tow-headed, Second Fifteen forward, overdue for his First Fifteen colours, and in aspect like an earnest, elderly horse'. Winton enjoys the respect of King (who is more sympathetically presented in the later stories)—and also, with a reservation, of the Head. 'Winton's only fault is a certain costive and unaccommodating virtue,' the Head says. 'So this comes very happily.'

Just what 'this' is takes some explaining. Winton, 'rigid and angular', had not come very well out of the Latin lesson—partly because, for the meaning of the one word he had not looked up during prep, he had rashly trusted to Beetle, whose approach to ancient languages tended to be imaginative rather than scholarly. Winton has partly retrieved himself—he has been all right on 'Well though he knew what the savage torturer was getting ready for him'—but his earlier howler has produced roars of laughter from the form, and this has upset his rather anxiously self-regarding nature. Matters are made worse when Beetle cheerfully mocks him: 'Don't be too virtuous. Don't brood over it. 'Twon't count against you in your future careeah.' (This adds to our sense of Winton's character; he is, as King calls him, 'prudential': anxious about his future, and 'virtuous' in order to safeguard it.) But now—and goaded in this way—Winton does a seemingly unaccountable, and certainly uncharacteristic, thing. He lets loose a live mouse in the form-room of Mr. Lidgett, the drawing-master. Winton is much too old to do such a thing with any propriety, and his fall from grace is the more evident because Mr. Lidgett, being no more than the drawing-master, is allowed very little power of punishment. Winton is at once overwhelmed with rather fussy remorse, declaring that he has played a cad's trick—and being, in fact, the virtuous Winton to rather a boring extent. Eventually he arrives in the Head's study—'penitent, perturbed, annoyed with himself'—and is told to produce five hundred lines of Virgil by tea-time. King is distressed, and with good reason. The seemingly mild penalty in fact masks something direly different. And it is because of this that the Head has said: 'So this comes very happily.'

At the United Services College—as it existed, and not

merely in Kipling's imagination—it was an absolute law that any boy who missed his football for any reason whatever, and had no written excuse, should be beaten by the Captain of Games. By setting an imposition that must be done during the time appointed for football, a master could be sure that a boy would be so beaten. And it is this sanction that the Head himself has invoked upon the virtuous Winton. As it happens, Winton shares a study with the Captain of Games, who is a boy of his own age, his cousin, and his closest friend. But it is a matter of honour that the law should be obeyed, and Winton (or, for that matter, his cousin, 'Pot' Mullins) obeys it—as Regulus had done. But he does not do so before, wrought upon by the rather tactless taunting of his fellows, he goes berserk (as Beetle calls it) and does a glorious amount of damage to everybody around him. As he has never fought before, this takes a good deal out of him, with the result that, seconds after the three strokes have been faithfully delivered, he astonishes Pot by stretching himself out on the window-seat of their study, and falling deeply and placidly asleep. This is the moment at which the Head's wisdom is presented as vindicated. He has acted only just in time, for Winton's 'Cap' has actually been delivered on the same day. He is still recognizably Winton; as he and Pot go off amicably to tea together, he is tiresomely disposed to reiterate once more his day's sins, and to speculate as to whether they will 'count against him'. But his 'moral joints' have been a little loosened up. Or so the Head hopes.

Perhaps it is excusable to misestimate 'Regulus' at a first encounter, and to feel that we are being asked to accept as valid for ourselves what are no more than the weird customs of some primitive tribe. But when we reconsider it, we may judge it—whether doctrinally sound or not—to be a more subtle fable than we had supposed, and certainly one based upon real penetration into the psychology of boyhood.

The most prominent theme in the Stalky stories is that of the punitive rag or practical joke; and the achieving of one or another feat in this kind tends to be accompanied by the release of orgiastic laughter. Both these elements are to be found widely dispersed throughout Kipling's work, often in stories keyed to a note of boisterous farce, but at times modulating into something quite different. Readers who dislike *Stalky & Co.*

are almost certain to condemn the whole species. Others will maintain that to omit notice of this kind of story is to ignore something which at least delighted Kipling and which is always likely to betray into momentary delight critics even of the most censorious temper.

Corrective physical humiliation in its more primitive form is already several times represented in the Indian stories. In 'The Judgment of Dungara' (*In Black and White*), the victims are a displeasing German missionary and his converts, who are persuaded by a slighted local priest to take up weaving operations with a fibre derived from the Nilgiri Nettle; the resulting garments, when donned, produce indescribable torments. 'A Friend's Friend' (*Plain Tales*) sticks to English *sahibs*. Objecting to a drunken character called Jevons, who has been offensive to ladies at a ball, they tie him up, smear him all over with anything sticky that is to hand, festoon him with cutlet-frills, roll him up in a carpet, and have him carted away with a load of furniture. 'He vanished utterly,' we are told. 'Perhaps he died and was thrown into the river.' This conjecture is no doubt intended as a pure joke. So is the whole manhandling of a drunken man. 'The Honours of War' is a much later story (*A Diversity of Creatures*) on a similar theme—only here the victim is conceived of as capable of salvation. A subaltern who has had the misfortune to spend three years at one of the ancient universities (and who has therefore added intolerable conceit to a natural ill-breeding) has been ragged by his fellows in some approved Kipling fashion, and is caddish enough to propose making the incident an occasion of public scandal. Fortunately, as it happens, no one less than Stalky himself (now a Lieutenant-Colonel) is around, and persuades the aggrieved young man to retort with cunningly contrived physical outrage of his own. Having achieved this, the subaltern apologizes handsomely to his fellow-officers for his previous unpleasing behaviour, and is then forgiven and received back into the favour of the mess. 'The Tie' (*Limits and Renewals*, 1932) is slighter—and here there is no salvation, since the victim is an outsider: a mere contractor who has offended an officers' mess by providing bad food. The officers corner him and slap his face in turn, choosing this mode of correction as the most humiliating; at a public school, it seems, it is what you would do to 'a chap who isn't big enough to beat'. The offender presumably understands this, since he has been at a public school himself. In fact he is seen to be wearing an Old School Tie, and this constrains his executioners to moderation. It is not easy to find merit in this story.

'Little Foxes' (*Actions and Reactions*, 1909) is a different matter. It is a story betraying, or rather parading, some of Kipling's most shocking prejudices, and it will not commend itself to persons instinctively respectful towards politicians or earnest in the cause of developing multiracial communities. It is exceedingly funny, all the same. The English Governor of some sizeable patch of the British Empire in the vicinity of Ethiopia discovers to his delighted amazement that there are foxes running wild in his territory. He at once imports a pack of hounds and establishes the Gihon Hunt. The natives are told what services undertaken for the Hunt will bring them reward, and what, on the contrary, will earn 'a most unmeasurable beating'—to wit, leaving unstopped on their land any 'earths' in which the foxes may take refuge. In this proposal the Governor has unwittingly discovered an admirably simple instrument of colonial administration. An earth on account of which one is beaten must at least be one's own earth, and as a consequence the beatings become so highly prized by the natives as constituting a species of title-deed that the Governor is able to establish a ceremony whereby a light and ceremonial switching with his hunting-crop becomes a convenient and recognized method of settling and confirming land claims. Meanwhile, back in England, a tiresome and offensive Member of Parliament has his leg pulled about the Gihon Hunt, which is described to him as a kind of mounted *Gestapo* practising the most horrible cruelties. Being a politician, he readily persuades other politicians to arm him with formidable powers, and he then hurries out to Gihon to put things right. He brings with him a stock of pamphlets for distribution, full of woolly-minded and vapid views of a liberal persuasion. In fact the distribution of these pamphlets can only produce dismay and anarchy, since they insist that the natives have undergone their ritual beatings in vain. Fortunately the personal appearance of the M.P. reminds everybody of a cherished hound in the Gihon pack which eventually went mad; moreover, in delivering a speech to the populace, interlarded with some scraps of the local language which he has got up for the purpose, he is tricked into making repeated use of some expression which is in fact deeply obscene. His efforts are drowned in universal laughter, whereupon he loses his temper, and attempts to give his interpreter a savage beating with his umbrella.

Other stories of this general character have an English setting. Most do not trespass beyond the bound of mere amusement, but a few, mainly of late composition, are elaborate structures in which farce is deployed against a background in which we glimpse the interplay of altogether more serious and sombre passions. 'Beauty Spots' (*Limits and Renewals*) involves painting spots on a pig called Angelique, an activity belonging to the world of children's comics, and ends with petty tyranny drowned by laughter. But when we come upon iron phrases in it—'the generation that tolerates but does not pity went away'—we know that they are meant to be there. It is so, too, with 'The Village that Voted the Earth was Flat' (*A Diversity of Creatures*). Sir Thomas Ingell is an unspeakably arrogant and uncivil landowner, and as a magistrate he carries these qualities with him to the local Bench. Sir Thomas is a small man as well as a nasty one, of no account whatever on the national scene. But having raised the just resentment of a group of far more powerful men, he finds that the entire Press and all the Music Halls of England have been organized to crush him. The story ends with the House of Commons reduced to paroxysms of laughter over Sir Thomas and all he stands for. But if we feel something disturbing in this vast punitive rag, and in the spectacle of engines of unlimited power being trained upon a single, rather absurd individual, we are again in the presence of something which Kipling has deliberately prepared for us. Men who conjure up laughter on this scale—we reflect, as we watch the High Court of Parliament itself swept into hysteria—are releasing a force they may be unable to control. It is true that Kipling's theory of laughter is of something essentially healthful. Indeed, there is a late short story, 'The Miracle of St. Jubanus' (*Limits and Renewals*), in which we are asked to believe that the cure of a French soldier, a neurotic war-casualty 'blasted, withered, dumb, a ghost that gnawed itself', is effected through a gigantic fit of mirth prompted by an absurd misadventure (it concerns the ill-behaviour of the *curé*'s umbrella) in the parish church. Nevertheless, Kipling's sense of the sacredness of laughter is also a sense of its power of disruption.

'Dayspring Mishandled' (*Limits and Renewals*) is the strangest of Kipling's stories of revenge achieved through the instrumentality of a joke. This joke takes years of painful labour to prepare. Its field is that of textual scholarship—which Kipling, as always with his background material, gets up with the greatest virtuosity. One scholar plants upon another, in order to discredit him, a forged fragment of a supposedly unknown Canterbury Tale by Chaucer. The plot darkens as it develops, until we are finally submerged in a world of pain and evil with which practical jokes seem to have little to do.

CHAPTER TEN

TWO WARS

AFTER THE FLIGHT from Vermont which followed the luckless feud with Beatty Balestier, the Kiplings had settled for a time at Torquay, on the south coast of Devon. The house they rented ought to have been delightful, but turned out to be mysteriously oppressive, and they stuck it for less than a year. We must suppose that low spirits had pursued them across the Atlantic. But so had the interest of people whose friendship they valued. Kipling corresponded regularly with Dr. Conland and C. E. Norton; and Carrie too wrote to Norton, as well as to May Cabot and others. The Nortons were, of course, eminently possessed of that full measure of earnestness in the pursuit of cultural things which the English, contemplating the perennial New England scene, are inclined for their own bad reasons to find amusing. There are signs of C. E. Norton's judging that, in verse at least, Kipling ought to be aiming higher. He may well have been right, and Carrie wrote placatingly—and perhaps with an amusing self-betrayal in the pronoun chosen:

> We are thoughtful over your admonition as to further verse-making. . . . We have set ourselves a more serious standard and have thrown several delightful things into the scrap-basket.

Kipling wrote, more robustly, that what he loved was 'the fun and riot of writing'. This was certainly true. We know that the Stalky stories were being written at about this time to the accompaniment of roars of laughter from their delighted author.

In corresponding with his American friends Kipling may have been disposed to play up his sense of nostalgia for their country. But he was certainly restless, and didn't much like his fresh view of his own countrymen—whom he was studying, he said, 'from the outside'. He even indulged a notion that he might go off to the Near East as a war correspondent. On the other hand, he was enjoying, more than he cared to admit, his wide acceptance as an important person. The Athenaeum Club elected him to membership under its celebrated Rule Two, which puts down a red carpet (metaphorically speaking) for the admission of a few individuals of the first eminence in public life. He visited Oxford, and although 'Varsity men seldom figure very favourably in his writing he was delighted by his reception:

> Three days later I went down to Oxford among the four hundred year old universities and dined with the tutors and so on at Balliol College. The boys cheered me so that the Master couldn't say grace and altogether I had a most wonderful time.

In the summer of 1897 the Kiplings moved to Rottingdean near Brighton, and remained there for five years. Relations and friends were numerous in the vicinity, so there was plenty of companionship for the children. It was in this period that Kipling began to earn himself a new kind of public status. He was still the writer who celebrated, both in prose and verse, the workaday world of the British Empire; who made vivid to readers at home the unassuming lives of the Queen's officers and servants far away. But people higher in the imperial hierarchy were becoming interested in him—and he in them. He now tended to see the problems of British policy—and in particular of colonial policy, which chiefly absorbed him—from the top; and to offer his fellow-countrymen, from time to time, augustly framed admonishments and encouragements through the medium of poems published in *The Times*—then, as now, the newspaper of the British governing class. Thus in June 1897, when some question of preferential tariffs was at issue with Canada, he sent to *The Times* a poem called 'Our Lady of the Snows', which begins:

> A Nation spoke to a Nation,
>   A Queen sent word to a Throne:
> 'Daughter am I in my mother's house.
>   But mistress in my own . . .'

A few days later, Kipling was lunching with the Colonial Premiers (soon to be the Dominion Premiers) in London. Several of these poems of statecraft were already behind him.

Kipling was to put much passionate conviction into this sort of thing. It is a quality which politicians, on the whole, fight shy of; and Kipling grew more and more at odds with them as the years went by. Nevertheless, he had authority with them, and was to retain it long after the literary critics had committed the grave folly of virtually dismissing him from notice. It was an authority that he exerted to startling effect upon the occasion of Queen Victoria's Diamond Jubilee in the summer of 1897.

The Jubilee, inevitably, was made the occasion of a great deal of national self-congratulation; and there appears to have been a fond belief that Kipling (as in Max Beerbohm's cartoon of him) would wave his little Union Jack with the rest. But Kipling's feelings about that sort of thing were such as we have seen expressed in the Stalky story, 'The Flag of their Country'. His position was, in fact, awkward. That he was the nation's poet was only the more apparent because, in the previous year, Lord Salisbury as Prime Minister had with some cynicism appointed the laughably incompetent Alfred Austin to be Poet Laureate. It was natural that Kipling should be urged to compose a Jubilee ode for *The Times*. According to one story, he did attempt something, but Jubilee Day, 22nd June, found him with nothing but a few stanzas—which he judged unsatisfactory—designed to carry the refrain 'Lest we forget'. He then went off for a fortnight to watch the Fleet on manœuvres. On returning, and while sorting through various recent papers, he threw the abandoned verses into a waste-paper basket. They were retrieved, with his leave, by Sallie Norton, then on a visit to the Kiplings; Kipling revised them in consultation with this young woman, his aunt Georgie Burne-Jones, and Carrie; and the next day 'Recessional' appeared in *The Times*. A recessional is the hymn sung at the conclusion of a religious service and while the clergy are retiring. The title therefore suggested that Kipling was providing a *coda* to the national celebration. He had not meant to be adroit—but nothing more adroit could have been conceived:

> The tumult and the shouting dies;
> The Captains and the Kings depart . . .

This was literally true; all sorts of grandees upon the world's stage had arrived for the Jubilee, and by now had packed their bags again.

> Far-called, our navies melt way;
> On dune and headland sinks the fire . . .

This, again, was fact: on Jubilee Day Kipling and Carrie had watched the bonfires fading along the south coast; and after the great Review the ships of the Grand Fleet had dispersed, a 'silent service', around the world, once more. England was left to think things over—and with not a little to remember in the way of 'frantic boast and foolish word'. Kipling had finally written a hymn about it all—clearly a hymn, since it could be sung to the tune of 'Eternal Father, strong to save . . .'—and had balanced the summons to 'an humble and a contrite heart' with the assertion that the Anglo-Saxon race (which included Sallie Norton, the heroine of the waste-paper basket) was by nature superior to 'lesser breeds without the Law'. Perhaps this is shocking, and there is certainly an element in 'Recessional' which liberal sentiment does not readily swallow. But nobody who has witnessed a great English national solemnity can be in any doubt about how the poem was received.

When Kipling took his family to winter in South Africa at the end of the Jubilee year it was as a person of consequence on the imperial stage, so that he at once made the acquaintance of the two most important men in Cape Town, Alfred Milner and Cecil Rhodes. Milner, a young man recently arrived as Colonial Secretary, was to prove very much in the tradition of the great English proconsuls, at once dispassionate in his handling of political issues and dedicated to the patient and unflagging pursuit of the objective laid down for him. This consisted essentially, on a long term view, in eliminating the independent Boer republics of the Transvaal and the Orange Free State, and establishing a wholly British South Africa. It is not now self-evident that it was a laudable idea, and in Great Britain as well as abroad plenty of people were to see the South African War, when it came, as a brutal crushing of small and independent peoples. The moral position, however, was not entirely simple. In the Transvaal, in particular, the Boers, while being a minority of the white population, permitted no share in political control to those *uitlanders*, of British origin for the most part, who were in fact the economic backbone of the country. Anybody persuaded of the need and possibility of progressive policies and the development of vast material resources over South Africa as a whole had a strong case for declaring that the Boers were an unamiable anachronism whose petty political tyrannies must be broken.

Cecil Rhodes believed this, and he at once commanded Kipling's respect. To this day Rhodes remains an enigmatic figure: a practical man and not a scrupulous one; and also an honourable dreamer in the service of large impersonal causes. It was self-evident to him that first a telegraph and then a railway must run from Cairo to the Cape; it was self-evident to him that men of his own race and kind must call or hale Africa out of savagery and into the new century. Kipling believed these things. It is true that our pomp of yesterday is one with Nineveh and Tyre, but the civilized must toil to spread their civilization, all the same. 'Clear the land of evil, drive the road and bridge the ford', we are enjoined in 'A Song of the English', and Kipling was to have no difficulty in seeing the Boer President, Paul Kruger, as very evil indeed:

> We shall take our station, dirt beneath his feet,
> While his hired captains jeer us in the street.
>
> Cruel in the shadow, crafty in the sun,
> Far beyond his borders shall his teachings run.
>
> Sloven, sullen, savage, secret, uncontrolled,
> Laying on a new land evil of the old.

There was to be a reckoning with President Paul Kruger. Meanwhile, Kipling went north to visit Rhodes's most remarkable creation but one: Rhodesia. It was an enormous territory, and had recently been 'pacified' by the destruction of the warlike Matabele—'machine guns', we are told, 'being used with terrible effect upon the enemy'. Now things were going ahead. Kipling was able to travel around on a bicycle hired in Bulawayo.

When the Kiplings returned to England in spring it was to hear of the outbreak of the Spanish-American war. Kipling had reason to feel concerned—and even to feel entitled to speak. The American Minister in London called upon him on the day he landed, and three days later the two men dined together with Rhodes, who had recently arrived in England. History had taken a small ironic turn—this in the sense that what might have begun in the Transvaal had begun in Cuba instead. There and in the Philippines, the United States had felt obliged to put an end to outmoded and reactionary forms of government, and had thus found itself for the first time confronted with a distinctively colonial problem.

It has to be remembered that, at this time, the British and American peoples supported between them incomparably the most important role in spreading the standards and achievements of modern Western civilization throughout the globe. In practical terms the British contribution had been the more important hitherto, but by now the population of the United States had surpassed that of Great Britain, and its production was increasing at a pace unprecedented in history. In the partnership of the 'Anglo-Saxon races' Kipling saw a great civilizing hope; in a memorable and ominous phrase he christened the job to be undertaken 'the White Man's burden'; and with his eye on the Philippines in particular he wrote a poem with that title, urging Americans not to hesitate in accepting their destiny. The result is a brilliantly executed harangue:

Take up the White Man's burden—
  Send forth the best ye breed—
Go bind your sons to exile
  To serve your captives' need;
To wait in heavy harness,
  On fluttered folk and wild—
Your new-caught, sullen peoples,
  Half-devil and half-child. . . .

Take up the White Man's burden—
  The savage wars of peace—
Fill full the mouth of Famine
  And bid the sickness cease;
And when your goal is nearest
  The end for others sought,
Watch Sloth and heathen Folly
  Bring all your hope to nought.

Take up the White Man's burden—
  Have done with childish days—
The lightly proffered laurel,
  The easy, ungrudged praise.
Comes now, to search your manhood
  Through all the thankless years,
Cold, edged with dear-bought wisdom,
  The judgement of your peers!

It was a message, not of very modest implication, from an old colonial power to a new. Theodore Roosevelt, who had fought as a volunteer in the Spanish War and was within a couple of years to be President of the United States, sent an advance copy of 'The White Man's Burden' to H. Cabot Lodge with the comment that it was 'rather poor poetry, but good sense from the expansionist standpoint'. This was in January 1899. By the end of that year the British Government had responded to an ultimatum from Kruger with a declaration of war. It was a war which was to be widely viewed, alike in America and Europe, as undertaken 'from the expansionist standpoint'.

The Kiplings were back in South Africa in January 1900. They were to winter there, in a house provided by Rhodes, in each successive year until 1908, always returning to England in the spring. Until the Treaty of Vereeniging in June 1902 signalled the capitulation of the Boers, Kipling, whether at home or in South Africa, was ceaselessly busy about the war. He raised a very large sum of money for the relief of soldiers' dependants simply by writing a single Music-Hall song, 'The Absent-Minded Beggar'; he built a drill-hall, formed a volunteer company, and organized a rifle-range at Rottingdean. In South Africa he was able to play, after a fashion, that part of war correspondent which had always haunted him; for a time he had a newspaper-office around him once more, the Commander-in-Chief having invited him to lend prestige to a paper issued to the troops by taking a place on its staff; at an action at Karee Siding (typical of scores of unsatisfactory and inconclusive engagements which the British had to fight) the man who above all others had written with genius of the English soldier for the first time saw troops under fire. The war inevitably prompted him to much writing both in prose and verse, but it cannot be said to have elicited any of his best work;

indeed, it was the completion of *Kim* that was the real literary achievement of these years.

Nevertheless, the Boer War had an immensely important influence on Kipling's thought. He had seen the British Army, whose poet he was, present before the world the appearance of a force ill-trained, ill-equipped, and ill-led; had seen it held up and hard-pressed by a few farmers who could ride and shoot. The men who could ride and shoot on the British side had come from Australia and New Zealand. This was humiliating. But far worse than present humiliation was the danger that lay ahead. The law of nations is the law of armed might. If things went on as they did, Great Britain, folded in a debilitating ease, would be like a defenceless house, its doors left wide open to whatever armed burglars cared to turn up. Already Germany was building a navy which was to have parity with the Grand Fleet itself. In the face of this situation Kipling wrote 'The Islanders':

> Then were the judgements loosened; then was
> your shame revealed,
> At the hands of a little people, few but apt
> in the field. . . .
> And ye vaunted your fathomless power, and ye
> flaunted your iron pride,
> Ere—ye fawned on the Younger Nations for the
> men who could shoot and ride!
> Then ye returned to your trinkets; then ye
> contented your souls
> With the flannelled fools at the wicket or the
> muddied oafs at the goals.

That the playing fields of Eton were precisely where future battles might be *lost* was a proposition taking some courage to enunciate. Kipling added, for good measure, that the gentry would find their pheasant-shooting not particularly useful 'when the raided coast-towns burn', and that the country's intellectuals were also a useless crowd, being 'arid, aloof, incurious, unthinking, unthanking, gelt'.

The cogency of Kipling's warning was to be proved twice within the succeeding half-century.

A few days after the signing of the Treaty of Vereeniging Kipling bought 'Bateman's', a stone-built Jacobean house with thirty-three acres of land at Burwash, an unfrequented village in Sussex. It was to be his home for the rest of his days. He was only thirty-six, and might almost have been called a young man rather than a middle-aged one; nevertheless, what he entered upon in this new house has distinguishably the character of later life. The visitors' book was to show plenty of coming and going in the years ahead, but nevertheless Kipling had begun a move into isolation. For a man so tenacious of memory and affection he was curiously prone to a closing of chapters behind him. India, where developments were not according to his ideas, he wrote off entirely, even declining invitations to join the royal party there during visits in 1903 and 1911. It was the same with South Africa; when Milner's policy was abandoned by a Liberal Government in 1905 he continued to winter in the country for a few years longer, and then abandoned it with the comment that 'the handing over of a higher civilization to a lower is a heart-breaking job'. Nor did he keep his American connections in repair, partly because his Boston friends had been disturbed by the tone of 'The White Man's Burden'. Naulakha was sold to the Cabots for a surprisingly small sum, perhaps because Beatty was threatening to dispute the title. For a time Kipling was enthusiastic about Canada, where he found a respect for law and order much superior to that in the United States. Politically he was moving to the extreme right, so that gradually it seemed as if he were speaking no longer for the working rank-and-file of the Empire, but for one section of the Conservative party. When eventually his cousin Stanley Baldwin became Prime Minister Kipling was called in to polish any of his speeches which it was judged would benefit from a literary flavour; and it appears that he had the distinction of writing for King George V the first address to the Nation and Commonwealth to be broadcast by a British sovereign. But by then Kipling had long since ceased to have any effective voice in public affairs.

In the literary world, too, Kipling's progress, from his early middle years, was towards isolation. He seems to have made little effort to get to know younger writers as they came along, and of his elder contemporaries and contemporaries he saw less and less. Henry James, a punctilious accorder of due visits, would sometimes come to stay, or pay a call. Thomas Hardy, who had once taken him house-hunting, appears to have dropped out of his life. Carrie, who came more and more to arrange Kipling's contacts, may not have realized that there was anything amiss here.

There was one exception—significant rather than notable—to this departure of literary people from the scene. Almost immediately upon coming to London Kipling had met Rider Haggard—and may even have learnt that, when the British annexed the Transvaal in 1877, it was Haggard who had run up the British flag in Pretoria. Something like fame had come to Haggard eight years later when, as an unsuccessful barrister, he had turned to the writing of popular romance with an African background, notably *King Solomon's Mines* and *She*. Kipling was as delighted by these exciting yarns as was any English schoolboy. From Vermont he wrote to Haggard declaring that it was *Nada the Lily* that had set him 'writing a lot of wolf-stories'. When they met again later it was evident that they had a great deal in common. Haggard believed in 'a divine right of a great civilizing people', and even held the same views as Kipling on the dangerous futility of professional cricket. Moreover, Haggard was by inheritance what Kipling by the purchase of Bateman's had become: an English landowner. He was a landowner, too, with a keen and informed interest in agricultural science, and was regularly appealed to as an authority. Kipling admired this very much; and in his correspondence with Haggard he will be found rather amusingly striving for his old 'knowing' note by way of keeping his end up in matters of cattlefeed and the like. Kipling also managed to admire Haggard's later writing, and spent much time collaborating with him in forming the plots of extravagant and imaginatively negligible romances. Kipling's attitude was quite uncritical, and it may have been this that led to Haggard's taking his own literary reputation a little too seriously. But there was small harm in this. And the friendship is almost the only one that Kipling can be seen as sustaining with real warmth during much of the later course of his life. This is no more than to say again that he was very devotedly a family man. His wife, son and daughter were enough for an immediate world; and beyond these, very close to his affections still, were his parents, soon to be old and ailing, and his sister, often sick in mind. What lay beyond that was essentially a world of acquaintances and associates: retired service people, dissident Tory politicians, influential journalists, with whom public affairs could be discussed—usually in a sombre and disillusioned way.

When John Kipling was born in 1897 Kipling had described him in a letter as 'one small craft recently launched from my own works'. And he added: 'The vessel at present needs at least 15 yrs for full completion but at the end of that time may be an efficient addition to the Navy, for which service it is intended.' Although the tone is humorous the act of dedication was serious enough, and in due course a famous Admiral, Sir John Fisher, offered to nominate John for a naval cadetship—as Fisher himself had been nominated, fifty years before, by the last survivor among Nelson's captains. There was something to stir the imagination in that. But it was not to be, for John's eyesight was early seen to fall short of the standard that would be required for the Navy. He was therefore sent to Wellington, the public school with the strongest military tradition at that time. In John's character there was nothing that his father, could he be conceived as opening his mouth on such a subject, would not have praised. Books, however, were not his strong point, and eventually he had to be taken away from Wellington and prepared for Sandhurst at a private crammer's (a proceeding which Stalky and his friends held in facile contempt). This was the state of affairs when the First World War broke out in August 1914. John, still just short of seventeen, went straight up to London to apply for a commission. Whether on the score of his age or his eyesight, he was turned down, and he then proposed trying to enlist as a private soldier. Had he thus entered the ranks, it is conceivable, though not likely, that he would be alive today. His father, however, appealed to Lord Roberts, who at once secured a nomination to his own crack regiment, the Irish Guards. John was in training by 14th September. In the summer of the following year—again because of his age—he had to obtain his father's permission to join the Second Irish Guards in France. On 22nd August Kipling, who had been touring the war zone and was now in Paris, wrote to John, and included (it was the old knowing Kipling, once more) some practical advice: 'Don't forget the beauty of rabbit netting overhead against hand-grenades. Even tennis netting is better than nothing.' We do not know whether John was able to lay his hand on any tennis netting. On 2nd October Kipling received a telegram from the War Office announcing that his son was wounded and missing. This was in the Battle of Loos, which cost the British 20,000 dead. There was a long period of hoping against hope (a poignant agony known in almost every English street) before John's survival had to be despaired of. His body was never recovered. It was more than two years before the Kiplings received a reliable account of the manner of his death. He had been shot through the head while attacking with his revolver a strongly held position deep in the enemy's defences.

Nobody acquainted with some of Kipling's stories and verses occasioned by the Boer War could be in any expectation that he would traverse the years 1914–1918 with no exhibition of bitterness and even hatred, directed alike against his country's enemies and (as he conceived them) its laggard allies—or for that matter such of his own countrymen in high places as he judged to be guilty of an ill direction of British arms. But this was something native in him, and present from the first. There is no evidence that his son's death further darkened for him the guilt of those he judged guilty. John had taken the road to which his father had pointed not John only but tens of thousands of English boys like him. For this is something of which we can be quite certain. The 'Temporary Second Lieutenants' who died by thousands and tens of thousands while leading and encouraging their men in the mud of Flanders were ruled by a code, fortified (if we like) by a myth, which Kipling had done as much to create as all the public schools of England put together. His personal sorrow was thus an impersonal sorrow as well.

In the years that followed the First World War Kipling undertook three public tasks. He compiled and edited, with labour and great care, the two volumes called *The Irish Guards in the Great War* (1923). This he owed directly to his son. He accepted office—the first he had ever held—as one of the Imperial War Graves Commissioners. He was active in all the decisions of this body, and was its sole authority upon what words, here and there about the globe, might most properly be engraved in stone. These were, in a sense, backward-looking tasks. He also became one of the Rhodes Trustees, administering the great educational fund into which Cecil Rhodes had poured all his wealth in the end.

CHAPTER ELEVEN

THE MATURE CRAFTSMAN

THERE IS A celebrated essay by Mr. Edmund Wilson called 'The Kipling that Nobody Read', and it is the achievement of this Kipling—an artist in full maturity—which remains to be considered. That people simply ceased reading Kipling during this phase of his career is, of course, rather a long way from being literally true. But as his art, in Mr. Wilson's words, 'became continually more skilful and intense' he certainly lost many of those readers who had enjoyed chiefly the simple, emphatic, and pictorial side of his writing. It is hard to imagine his own William, for example, making much of the subtle and elusive clues which are the reader's sole guide through some of the later stories. What may appear surprising is that Kipling entirely failed to impress in a new way either the professional critics or the more sophisticated 'common readers'. Yet there is nothing really perplexing about this, since the history of literature and the arts presents many illustrations of the fact that a man's early achievement, if striking enough, may 'type' him for good, so that few, even among the more sensitive and discerning, must notice or admire what later generations may acknowledge as an enlarged and deepened vision. Rembrandt is a classic instance of this.

Further factors were at play. Kipling lived and worked in privacy, and it would not have occurred to him to cultivate the society of persons likely to be influential in recommending him to the continued regard of the public. Again—and this is more important—a great deal remained unchanged alike in Kipling's tone and in his fundamental assumptions. His later writing, it is true, can now be discerned as bearing the stamp of suffering to which no clue is afforded us by any word of Kipling's own—and only an imperfect clue by what we have come to know of his personal history. The fruit of this suffering is compassion, disillusion, and courage to face nakedly 'the gods of things as they are'. Yet these qualities are brought to us still defiantly parcelled up with passions and prejudices as old as Beetle's while he wields the cricket stump, or the brash young Anglo-

Indian journalist's when he believes himself to descry the pitiful inadequacy of San Francisco's seaward defences. To the end, that is to say, Kipling retains the power and will to irritate all those 'liberal' sentiments of which he strenuously disapproved. Let us consider something of this sustained power to irritate through the medium of the short story.

'An Habitation Enforced' (*Actions and Reactions*) will make a good beginning. A wealthy American business man, George Chapin, falls seriously ill 'at the very hour his hand was outstretched to crumple the Holtz and Gunsberg Combine', and his doctors pack him and his wife Sophie off to Europe for a couple of years. They drift around, staring at the things tourists stare at, 'from the North Cape to the Blue Grotto at Capri'. Chapin feels frustrated, and longs to get back to work. It is true, he tells Sophie, that he has between four and five million:

> 'But it isn't the money. You know it isn't. It's the principle. How could you respect me? You never did, the first year after we married, till I went to work like the others. Our tradition and upbringing are against it. We can't accept *those* ideals.'

The Chapins go to England, and an acquaintance sends them to lodge in a farmhouse in one of the southern counties, promising that they will find there 'the genuine England of folklore and song'. This is still tourist-brochure stuff—but what the Chapins actually find is an empty and dilapidated Georgian mansion, along with an estate of half a dozen neglected farms. The house is called Friars Pardon, and when Sophie falls in love with it her husband buys it—reflecting that he 'could double the value of the place in six months'. Actually George Chapin is almost as sensitive as his wife to the social pitfalls surrounding wealthy Americans who buy English landed properties. But they learn quickly, for the most part from their servants and tenants. On one occasion, just before their purchase of the estate, Sophie, entering the derelict home farm, finds the old man who lives there sitting dead in his chair. She feels that she must not run for help, but must watch with the body until somebody else happens to turn up. A few days later, she also feels that such a newcomer as herself (although now become the lady of the manor) would be taking a liberty is she attended his funeral. Much of this sort of thing in the

Chapins is marked and silently approved. Moreover, since they are well-bred and unassuming, they are received by the local gentry—a privilege denied an even wealthier new-comer, Mr. Sangres, who is Brazilian and vulgar.

When the Chapins go to church for the first time as the owners of Friars Pardon they are ushered with ceremony into the Pardon's Pew. Sophie finds this an ordeal—but it is an ordeal with a strange culmination:

> '*When the wicked man turneth away.*' The strong alien voice of the priest vibrated under the hammer-beam roof, and a loneliness unfelt before swamped their hearts, as they searched for places in the unfamiliar Church of England service. The Lord's Prayer—'Our Father, *which* art'—set the seal on that desolation. Sophie found herself thinking how in other lands their purchase would long ere this have been discussed from every point of view in a dozen prints. . . . Here was nothing but silence—not even hostility! The game was up to them; the other players hid their cards and waited. Suspense, she felt, was in the air, and when her sight cleared, saw indeed, a mural tablet of a footless bird brooding upon the carven motto, 'Wayte awhyle—wayte awhyle'.
>
> At the Litany George had trouble with an unstable hassock, and drew the slip of carpet under the pew-seat. Sophie pushed her end back also, and shut her eyes against a burning that felt like tears. When she opened them she was looking at her mother's maiden name, fairly carved on a blue flagstone on the pew floor:
>
> Ellen Lashmar. ob. 1796. aetat. 27.

Wondering at this strange coincidence, Sophie writes to an aunt for information on her family history:

> Her Aunt Sydney of Meriden (a badged and certificated Daughter of the Revolution to boot) answered her inquiries with a two-paged discourse on patriotism, the leaflets of a Village Improvement Society, of which she was president, and a demand for an overdue subscription to a Factory Girls' Reading Circle.

Whether or not Aunt Sydney's ignorance is to be judged plausible, it is through some transatlantic correspondence among very humble folk that the truth appears and is revealed to Sophie. Her mother's family did indeed come from these parts, and were of an ancient and honourable stock. Socially speaking, Sophie now has a trump card, but she remembers the family motto, 'Wayte awhyle', and refrains from playing it. She has her reward. When her first son is born, an august neighbour, Lady Conant, who has also worked out the truth, sends her an antique christening mug which had been in the Lashmar family for generations—simply adding as a postscript to her note: 'How quiet you've kept about it all!'

'What does she mean about our keeping quiet?' George Chapin asks his wife.

> Sophie's eyes sparkled. 'I've thought that out too. We've got back at the English at last. Can't you see that *she* thought that we thought my mother's being a Lashmar was one of those things we'd expect the English to find out for themselves, and that's impressed her?' She turned the mug in her white hands, and sighed happily. ' "Wayte awhyle—wayte awhyle". That's not a bad motto, George. It's been worth it.'

To 'An Habitation Enforced' there is appended a poem, 'The Recall', which begins:

> I am the land of their fathers,
> In me the virtue stays;
> I will bring back my children
> After certain days.
>
> Under their feet in the grasses
> My clinging magic runs.
> They shall return as strangers,
> They shall remain as sons.

Let us leave this story without comment for the moment, and turn to 'My Son's Wife' (*A Diversity of Creatures*). This too is about somebody whose ways of feeling, thinking and behaving are changed by the impact of English country life. In one respect Frankwell Midmore has less far to go than the Chapins, since he is an Englishman. But essentially he has to go further. George Chapin, although represented at the start as suffering more than bodily sickness as a consequence of the pressures of a sterile competitive life, is a mature and straight personality, and his wife owns as alert a sensitiveness as one of Henry James's American heroines. Midmore, on the contrary, has all the appearance of being a hopelessly rubbishing character. His main activity, fairly broadly intimated to us, is an undignified sexual promiscuity carried on beneath the cloak of disinterested moral and social reform:

> He and a few friends had rearranged Heaven very comfortably, but the reorganization of Earth, which they called Society, was even greater fun. It demanded Work in the shape of many taxi-rides daily; hours of brilliant talk with brilliant talkers; some sparkling correspondence . . . and a fair number of picture-galleries, tea-fights, concerts, theatres, music-halls, and cinema shows; the whole trimmed with love-making to women whose hair smelt of cigarette-smoke. Such strong days sent Frankwell Midmore back to his flat assured that he and his friends had helped the World a step nearer the Truth, the Dawn, and the New Order.

We have met these objectionable people before. They are the 'long-haired things' of those first contemptuous verses sent back from London to the *Civil and Military Gazette*. They are, for that matter, the *Bandar-log*.

Midmore unexpectedly inherits a house and some land in the country, and we are given his first 'sparkling' letter about it. He has nothing but ridicule for the place and its people, and is determined to sell out as soon as a purchaser can be found. But then his current love-affair collapses—with rather more serious nervous consequences than one might judge probable. He takes refuge in his new house, and is cared for by an old family retainer called Rhoda, who remembers him as a child:

> It was not a dignified entry, because when the door was unchained and Rhoda exclaimed, he took two valiant steps into the hall and then fainted—as men sometimes will after twenty-two hours of strong emotion and little food.
>
> 'I'm sorry,' he said when he could speak. He was lying at the foot of the stairs, his head on Rhoda's lap.

'Your 'ome is your castle, sir,' was the reply in his hair. 'I smelt it wasn't drink. You lay on the sofa till I get your supper.'

She settled him in a drawing-room hung with yellow silk, heavy with the smell of dead leaves and oil lamp. Something murmured soothingly in the background and overcame the noises in his head. He thought he heard horses' feet on wet gravel and a voice singing about ships and flocks and grass. It passed close to the shuttered bay window.

> But each will mourn his own, she saith,
> And sweeter woman ne'er drew breath
> Than my son's wife, Elizabeth . . .
> Cusha——cusha——cusha——calling.

The singer, the daughter of a neighbour returning from hunting, is the girl Midmore will marry when his full salvation is accomplished. To detail in terms of psychological realism the course of such a salvation is beyond the scope of a short story, and also beyond Kipling's range. So the thing is done in terms of a bold shorthand. Midmore finds himself reading the hunting novels of Surtees and recognizing his new neighbours in them; he secretly learns to shoot and ride; he finds satisfaction in countering the wiles of his tenant at the home farm and getting on terms with him. This would not in itself produce anything very memorable: only a fable about an English and grown-up Harvey Cheyne. But Kipling also has other devices at his command ('horses' feet on wet gravel'); and the climax of the story comes when a dam bursts, and the stream which has murmured in the background of the story overflows its banks with an effect both of practical challenge and symbolic purification. Already, while his new life has been gaining on him, Midmore has viewed his former associates with clearer sight and judged that their 'old tricks were sprouting in the old atmosphere like mushrooms in a dung-pit'.

Both these stories—'An Habitation Enforced' and 'My Son's Wife'—require a certain radical sympathy in the reader if they are not to appear bullying performances. They are emphatic statements of persuasions which can readily present themselves as prejudices; we may feel that we are being faced with arguments in which one side is allowed to have things all its own way. Yet they do faithfully reflect elemental facts of human life, and they touch us at depths of our own nature where the 'clinging magic' does run. Nor must we be misled by the mere social overtones of the stories. The fact that Sophie Chapin is herself a Lashmar draws only trivial significance as affecting her place in relation to an existing English class-structure; what Sophie (like Midmore) is really discovering is that the present must acknowledge and contain the past, if life itself is to be rightly known as a sacred flame. Both stories, then, deal with something very primitive. So, in a simpler and even more impressive way, does a third. It, too, has a brook in it. Indeed, it is called 'Friendly Brook' (*A Diversity of Creatures*).

Here there are no social complications whatever. The characters are all simple countryfolk, such as would be called 'peasants' on the continent of Europe. Two old men are hedging and ditching—and near by there is a brook beginning to flood. In the course of their talk we simply learn why another countryman, Jim Wickenden, insists on building his hay-stack so low down in the meadow that the brook looks like sweeping it away as it swells. One of the old men rounds off the tale:

> 'Well, well! Let be how 'twill, the brook was a good friend to Jim. I see it now. I allus *did* wonder what he was gettin' at when he said that, when I talked to him about shiftin' the stack. "You dunno everythin'," he ses, "an' if she's minded to have a snatch at my hay, *I* ain't settin' out to withstand her." '

The good turn which the brook did Jim Wickenden was to drown his enemy, a city blackguard who had the legal power to take away Wickenden's beloved (although not very loving) adopted daughter, and who had been practising blackmail on the strength of this. Here the story in itself is, in a sense, nothing; what is remarkable is the power of the dialogue to carry us into remote modes of feeling, in which it is taken for granted that the brook has its own life, and is fitly to be rewarded and propitiated with a 'snatch' of hay, should it be minded to take one.

The pagan feeling commanded in 'Friendly Brook' derives

its effectiveness, at least in part, from being given expression in a tale with a contemporary setting; the old men who discourse in it could have been met with in any corner of Kipling's Sussex, and might indeed be so met with today. There are other stories in which the historical imagination operates without a 'frame' of this sort, and notable among these is 'The Eye of Allah' (*Debits and Credits*). The setting is an English monastery in the thirteenth century, and we are introduced to an artist, John of Burgos, 'burnishing a tiny boss of gold in his miniature of the Annunciation for his Gospel of St. Luke'. This, and later other of John's illuminations, are exhibited to us in brilliant detail, and we find eventually that the effect of the story depends upon this. John travels about Europe, and will presently be revisiting Spain; we are told, again in detail, of the various pigments and rare substances he is commissioned to bring back for the use of the monastery's Scriptorium—and also of drugs and salves which both the Infirmarian and the Abbot Stephen himself (for Stephen is passionately interested in medicine) similarly ask for. John, at the moment, is wholly absorbed in the problem of visualizing and depicting devils and evil spirits in inexhaustible variety, for without these how shall his Great Luke deal worthily with the Miracle of the Magdalene and the Miracle of the Gadarene swine? John's prompting is wholly the artist's; to him men are 'but matter for drawings'; when once he has achieved his devils, devils will cease to interest him. He does achieve them, bringing back from Spain 'wholly a new sort'. Kipling's description of them, leading our mind gropingly as it does towards the heart of the story, is surely one of his most astonishing achievements:

> Some devils were mere lumps, with lobes and protuberances —a hint of a fiend's face peering through jelly-like walls. And there was a family of impatient, globular devillings who had burst open the belly of their smirking parent, and were revolving desperately toward their prey. Others patterned themselves into rods, chains and ladders, single or conjoined, round the throat and jaws of a shrieking sow, from whose ear emerged the lashing, glassy tail of a devil that had made good his refuge. And there were granulated and conglomerate devils, mixed up with the foam and slaver where the attack was fiercest. . . .

> The border to the picture was a diaper of irregular but balanced compartments or cellules, where sat, swam, or weltered, devils in blank, so to say—things as yet uninspired by Evil—indifferent, but lawlessly outside imagination. Their shapes resembled, again, ladders, chains, scourges, diamonds, aborted buds, or gravid phosphorescent globes—some well-nigh star-like.

It is the Infirmarian who sees the relationship between border and picture: 'These lower shapes in the bordure may not be so much hellish and malignant as models and patterns upon which John has tricked out and embellished his proper devils among the swine above there!'

But where has John *seen* his models? The answer is: through the eye of what we should now call a microscope—an instrument of 'art optical' which he has obtained from a Moorish source, and which he now produces and places on the Abbot's after-table. The after-table is important to the total effect produced by the story. Stephen has been entertaining distinguished guests to dinner in his parlour; John and a few of the brethren have been bidden to meet them; it is at the after-table that the company takes its place for dessert: 'dates, raisins, ginger, figs, and cinnamon-scented sweetmeats set out, with the choicer wines'. This touch brings us very close to these thirteenth-century people; in polite society—aristocratic, learned or ecclesiastical—manners and customs do not much change (Kipling, as a matter of fact, must have met something very like this scene when he 'dined with the tutors and so on at Balliol College'); and we thus have rather remote habits of mind telescoped with manners, and a mode of conversation, which are familiar.

Soon the whole company is looking in turn through the lens of the microscope at a drop of puddle water from the monastery roof. Thomas the Infirmarian's mind takes a leap at a tremendous truth. 'As in the water, so in the blood must they rage and war with each other. . . . Think on it again! Here's the Light under our very hand!' Earlier in the evening Abbot Stephen has taken off his ring and dropped it into a silver cup—this in token that, for the time, he is simply a gentleman in the society of his equals. He puts his ring on again, and takes the microscope. He has known about the invention already, having been on an unsuccessful Crusade and held captive by the Saracens. He knows that 'man stands ever between two Infinities—of greatness and littleness'. But he knows, too, that in the Europe of the Mediaeval Church John's microscope is like an untimely birth, and anybody who appears to discern a million devils in a drop of water will merely go to the stake. The Infirmarian pleads: 'The little creatures shall be sanctified—sanctified to the service of His sick.' But Stephen knows what he must do. He asks John for his dagger, and smashes the microscope with its hilt.

The power of this great story cannot be adequately suggested in summary and quotation, since it derives in large part from the detail poured into it from a vivid and concretizing imagination. But at least it can be seen as a story deliberately inviting us to look into the future as well as the past. In the future, as at the present, science will offer men gifts they are unready for.

John, the artist in 'The Eye of Allah', is uninterested in doing the same thing twice; and Kipling declares himself to have had a compact with his Daemon never simply to follow up a success. (It was the Daemon, incidentally, who bade him, when 'The Eye of Allah' wouldn't come right, 'treat it as an illuminated manuscript', thus turning failure into success.) There is a rule here not easy for a prolific writer of short stories to keep, but Kipling commonly contrived to find at least a new slant on familiar material. 'The Church that was at Antioch' (*Limits and Renewals*) is another exercise of the historical imagination, being a close-up and intimate view of St. Peter and St. Paul wrestling with the situation briefly recounted in the eleventh chapter of the Epistle to the Galatians. But the events are shown us through the eyes of a young Roman officer, Valens, who has all the firmness, tact and tolerance which a first-class English subaltern might be expected to show in face of some more or less incomprehensible communal squabble in British India. The effect is contrived in the main by setting Valens and his uncle the Prefect talking in an idiom which constantly hints such a modern analogy. '*My* objection to fancy religions,' the Prefect says, 'is that they mostly meet after dark, and that means more work for the Police.' And, again: 'I've got to see Paulus and Petrus when they come back, and find out what they've decided about their infernal feasts. Why can't they all get decently drunk and be done with it?' This in itself would make only a superficial achievement. The story takes depth from the contrasted characters of Peter and Paul, and from a great moment at which Peter, hitherto troubled, hesitant, and apparently out of his depth, suddenly, and in a flash of spiritual perception, towers over the accomplished, intellectual, and commanding Apostle to the Gentiles. Moreover, Valens, when mortally wounded on duty, lays upon his uncle an injunction to mercy and forgiveness. 'Don't be hard on them,' he says. 'They get worked up. . . . They don't know what they are doing.' The echo of Christ's words gives us a sudden sense of a whole pagan world moving unknowingly towards one of the new 'fancy religions'.

Kipling himself was not a man who found forgiveness easy. That he was incapable of 'personal hate' we may believe; there is, as we have seen, his own word for it, and he was not a man who would record about himself any untruth whatever. Political animus, often bitter and deep, was another matter. Throughout his adult life there was seldom a time when he was quite safe from it. In particular his country's involvement in war was liable at once to trouble and to barb his art. 'A Sahib's War' and 'The Comprehension of Private Copper' (*Traffics and Discoveries*) are two stories prompted by the conflict with the Boers both of which hold something disturbingly unassimilated into the imaginative structure aimed at. A third, 'The Captive' (*Traffics and Discoveries*) is better; it is about an American inventor, Laughton O. Zigler, who has been interned by the British after equipping the Boers with a new type of field-gun. Zigler is allowed a fair run for his money—less because Kipling has any liking for him than because his sardonic American manner affords his creator an admirable medium in which to convey his own scorn and anger over the large incompetence of the British campaign. Zigler turns up again in 'The Edge of the Evening' (*A Diversity of Creatures*), a story first published in 1913, and which serves curiously as a prologue to Kipling's writing about the Great War which began a year later. It instances again the uncertainty of Kipling's feelings towards America.

Zigler, having acquired great wealth, has rented a very splendid English country-house, and filled it with guests from among his compatriots. These are far from sympathetically regarded; nor is Zigler himself, as long as he is in this *milieu*. It turns out, however, to be unimportant: a 'frame' for the main story, which is recounted by Zigler himself. He tells how, returning from his private golf-course with three English guests, he finds an aeroplane in his park. It has grounded while being flown by two German spies—and it is another invention of Zigler's, the Rush Silencer, which makes technically possible what they have been about: 'a bird's-eye telephoto-survey of England for military purposes'. We have at least to admit that Kipling is looking faithfully into the future here. But the rest of the story is implausible. The grounded spies, in order to have some chance of escape, at once attempt to kill their discoverers —but in fact their discoverers kill them: Zigler braining one with a golf-club, and an English high-court judge breaking the neck of the other with a lethal football tackle. Between them they hoist the bodies back into the plane which Zigler gets going with its controls so set that it will disappear into the English Channel. We are left with the impression that Zigler has acted less badly in marketing his silencer where he can than has the British Government in not being alert to secure it. We are also told that Zigler's English companions have placed themselves in a dangerous position, since their Government would not back them up if the fatal incident became public. The latter part of this story is admirably told, but we may feel that only an impatience to express political feeling would have hurried Kipling into a recital of improbabilities which could find acceptance only in a boys' magazine.

The most famous, or notorious, of Kipling's stories of the First World War is 'Mary Postgate' (*A Diversity of Creatures*), published in 1915. This too has an aeroplane in it, and two dead men. The first of these is Wynn Fowler, who went straight into the Flying Corps and got himself killed in a trial flight. Wynn had been an unlovely and graceless orphan, brought up by an aunt who cared little for him, and in his turn caring little for his aunt's paid 'companion', Miss Postgate, a dim-seeming woman who had been devoted to him, and whom, whether as boy or young man, he had never treated other than with breezy contempt. There is only Miss Postgate to be affected by his death:

> 'I never expected anything else,' said Miss Fowler; 'but I'm sorry it happened before he had done anything.'

The room was whirling round Mary Postgate, but she found herself quite steady in the midst of it.

'Yes,' she said. 'It's a great pity he didn't die in action after he had killed somebody.'

This sounds the dire note that is to come. Miss Postgate has the grim experience of chancing upon a child killed by a German bomb. Hard upon this, and while destroying in the garden incinerator Wynn's old toys, books, motoring journals and other personal possessions, she comes upon something else: a wounded man, 'in a uniform something like Wynn's'. He is an injured German airman, and he begs for help. Miss Postgate returns to the house, not for help but for a revolver. She has no need to use it. The man is groaning in his death-agony. 'Stop that!' Mary says, and stamps her foot. 'Stop that, you bloody pagan!' It is Wynn's sort of language. The man dies. That evening, Miss Fowler notices that her dim and repressed companion is looking, for once, 'quite handsome'.

It is easy to see that in 'Mary Postgate', as in one or two other war-stories which are less successful, Kipling begins from a passion of hate which he believes himself to share with his countrymen at large: a hate that is 'impersonal' in the sense of being directed not against an individual but against the evil-doing of the German nation. He even adds as tailpiece a poem called 'The Beginnings':

> It was not part of their blood,
> It came to them very late
> With long arrears to make good,
> When the English began to hate. . . .

But the *story* is not about the English beginning to hate, nor about Kipling beginning to hate, either. It is about something that happens to a particular woman when wrought upon by forces some of which she is quite unconscious of. This is what makes 'Mary Postgate' not merely a shattering story but a tragic story as well—one full of pity and terror. For nowhere else in Kipling are we so powerfully confronted with a horror which we are made to recognize as proceeding from an authentic exploration of human character in depth. All the emotion behind the story has been transfused into its action. Dreadful though it be, this is why it remains a work of art.

'The Gardener' (*Debits and Credits*) is another war-story about a woman, and one looking forward, in some respects, to the final phase of Kipling's work. Its key word, spoken once only, is 'compassion'. Helen Turrell has had an illegitimate son, Michael; and she has cleverly contrived to avert scandal, although at the cost of living out a lie. When her pregnancy could no longer be concealed she had gone to the South of France, invented various explanations to account for her long absence, and returned with the baby and the assertion that she has adopted the child of a brother who had lately died in India. The story is so told by Kipling that we may ourselves be misled by the untruth as we read—and on a rereading (so subtle is his narrative art) we cannot be certain whether or not Helen's friends and neighbours have similarly been deceived. When war breaks out Michael Turrell gains a commission, is thrown into the line after the Battle of Loos, and is soon posted as missing. Later (unlike John Kipling) his body is recovered and identified, and Helen eventually goes to visit his grave in a vast military cemetery in Flanders. In her hotel she meets another English woman who tells an improbable story of frequent visits to the cemetery simply on behalf of bereaved friends, but who then breaks down and confesses that it is to the grave of one whose mistress she had been that she is drawn back again and again:

> 'I'm *so* tired of lying. Tired of lying—always lying—year in and year out. When I don't tell lies I've got to act 'em and I've got to think 'em, always. *You* don't know what that means. . . . I *can't* go to him again with nobody in the world knowing.'

Helen tries to comfort this woman, but without admitting her own secret, so that the woman is obscurely repelled by her insincerity, and repulses her.

The next day Helen makes her way through the thousands and thousands of graves. She loses her bearings, and looks around for help:

> A man knelt behind a line of headstones—evidently a gardener, for he was firming a young plant in the soft earth. She went towards him, her paper in her hand. He rose at her

approach and without prelude or salutation asked: 'Who are you looking for?'

'Lieutenant Michael Turrell—my nephew,' said Helen slowly and word for word, as she had many thousands of times in her life.

The man lifted his eyes and looked at her with infinite compassion before he turned from the fresh-sown grass toward the naked black crosses.

'Come with me,' he said, 'and I will show you where your son lies.'

When Helen left the Cemetery she turned for a last look. In the distance she saw the man bending over his young plants; and she went away, supposing him to be the gardener.

In St. John's Gospel it is Mary Magdalen who supposes that the risen Christ 'must be the gardener'.

After writing 'The Church that was at Antioch' Kipling had not done with St. Peter and St. Paul. They appear severally in two sharply contrasting stories in his final collected volume, *Limits and Renewals*. 'The Manner of Men' is almost a nautical companion piece to the earlier story, being based upon the voyage and shipwreck described in the twenty-seventh chapter of *The Acts of the Apostles*. Here is a wonderfully convincing close-up view of seafaring in the ancient Mediterranean, carrying for us echoes from as far back as 'The Finest Story in the World'. To the mariners gossiping in these pages, Paul is no more than an odd philosopher, casually encountered; or rather he is at once this and a little man of unaccountable and unforgettable power.

'On the Gate' presents a very different Peter from the struggling saint of 'The Church that was at Antioch'. He now holds the keys of Heaven, and it is in Heaven that the story is set. Kipling was not a professing Christian, and there is something disconcerting at first—in appearance, indeed, almost frivolous—in his presentation of Death and Judgement, Salvation and Damnation, as matters transacting themselves through the machinery of something like an earthly Government Department. The story has a sub-title, 'A Tale of '16', and what we are shown is this machinery almost breaking down under the strain imposed upon it by the mounting war casualties of that year. Only Peter himself can cut through the red tape which, hour by hour, impedes the operation, and we are tempted to see him at once as a first-class Indian Civil Servant. The similitude is enhanced by his situation. Above him is a remote and inscrutable Power, not unlike the Government of India. Below him, and flooding in upon him, are helpless and driven millions. Like Scott who milked the goats in 'William the Conqueror', he must do what he can. But he is the authentic Peter of the Gospels in that he is the disciple of Christ (Who is not mentioned in the story), dedicating his will and intellect to an endless labour of mercy. The letter killeth, but the spirit giveth life; and Peter's job is really to circumvent the letter with all the guile of an experienced subordinate. It is this, rather than the lightness of fantasy and constantly hovering comedy, that imports something equivocal into the story. What Kipling himself saw as overarching this earth was not Heaven, but a void—and into that void he is here injecting something for which his heart hungers, but which is unsanctioned by his belief. There is a point at which Peter is made to cry out 'Samuel Two, Double Fourteen'. When we make the reference, we find the words of the Wise Woman of Tekoah. King David has been at fault in not calling home again his banished son. For it is otherwise with God: 'For we must needs die, and are as water spilt on the ground, which cannot be gathered up again; neither doth God respect any person; yet doth he devise means, that his banished be not expelled from him.' Kipling's story has the validity of poetry, not of theological belief. Peter, hard at work wresting the frame of things to 'devise means', has the limitations of something merely yearned for, not known. Yet 'On the Gate' is a deeply serious story. And St. Peter is its hero essentially because (to make one final return to 'William the Conqueror') he is among those 'who do things'. This places the fable in the full stream of Kipling's final writings. In these the constant threat is of acquiescence in hopeless, because passive, suffering. Kipling casts actively about for help and healing to the end.

The theme of healing is not confined entirely to Kipling's last period. It makes an appearance (in a sufficiently crude form) in as early a story as 'The Mark of the Beast'; in one or two places in *Puck of Pook's Hill;* and in a curious story called

'The House Surgeon' in *Actions and Reactions*. It will be remembered how the Kiplings, on returning from Vermont, found something mysteriously depressing in what appeared to be a delightful house at Torquay. In the actual house the mysterious blight seems to have been permanent, since Kipling found it just as bad when he revisited it thirty years later. But in 'The House Surgeon' such a house undergoes a cure. Its manner of afflicting with an unaccountable depression all who live there is found to be occasioned by their telepathic rapport with a former inmate who believes that her sister committed suicide in it. When the belief is proved to be erroneous the house ceases to be depressing.

This is a trivial story, but has interest as hovering between the supernatural and theories of psychopathology and psychotherapy which were to become increasingly current during the first quarter of the twentieth century. There is no evidence that Kipling knew much about Freud (whose *Die Traumdeutung* appeared in 1900); it is unlikely that he would have heard him talked about by the eminent and conservative English physicians who were among his acquaintances in later life; and there is much in Freud's ideas which he would have violently disliked. Nevertheless, certain of the stories seem to touch on Freudian psychotherapy as it came to be popularly conceived: some traumatic experience which has been 'repressed' is successfully restored to consciousness and confronted in a fashion from which a cure results. Kipling's tentative explorations here are likely to suffer from our associating them with mediocre novels and films which make facile play with this kind of thing. Some of them are remarkable, nevertheless. A pre-war story called 'In the Same Boat' (*A Diversity of Creatures*) is an example. Here a man and a woman have severally consulted their doctors when suffering from constant and insupportable nightmares. Manœuvred into each other's company on a railway journey, they establish a sympathetic relationship from which each derives strength and support, until finally it is discovered that the mother of each suffered some alarming experience during pregnancy. The result of this pre-natal illumination is 'unspeakable relief'. We are not very convinced by this story (in which we discern a distant relationship with 'The Brushwood Boy'). But it has a curious historical interest, and at the same time points forward to related post-war stories in which we feel Kipling's imagination to be much more deeply engaged.

A few of these stories are very obscure, particularly when they continue to hover indecisively between a psychological and a supernatural interpretation of their material. Thus 'The Dog Hervey' (*A Diversity of Creatures*) is a tale, or fantasy, on the true meaning of which there is still no agreement. Miss Sichliffe is an unattractive maiden lady, whom nobody has ever much liked except a wealthy man who has, however, disappeared from her life. Miss Sichliffe now loves only a dog (an unattractive dog), and eventually the Spiritual Form of this dog (as the poet Blake might have called it) appears to her former lover in circumstances not in themselves edifying—but with the consequence that a subsequent chain of events reunites the lovers, and they are married. The oblique and opaque character of 'The Dog Hervey' seems to reflect some area of its creator's mind resistant to the power of his art. Kipling wrote only one other story which is at once haunting and hopelessly mysterious. This is the much earlier 'Mrs. Bathurst' (*Traffics and Discoveries*), the theme of which appears to be sexual passion in its destructive aspect.

There is another dog in one of the late stories of healing, 'The Woman in his Life' (*Limits and Renewals*). John Marden, a sapper during the war, has returned from some stiff experiences —below ground and above—and has rapidly built up a flourishing engineering business. Quite suddenly he suffers a severe nervous breakdown, and this worsens when he takes refuge in drink. 'A Fear leaped out of the goose-fleshed streets of London between the icy shop-fronts, and drove John to his flat.' His condition grows yet worse, so that he becomes subject to hallucinations; among these is a small black dog, pressed against the skirting-board of his room; he believes that if the animal leaves this position the whole universe will come crashing down. Marden's manservant, also an ex-soldier, introduces a real black dog into the flat, a dwarf Aberdeen bitch. Marden, now that the spectral dog has become a real dog ('the woman in his life' is in fact the bitch Dinah), begins to recover. Eventually Dinah, by a strange chance, is trapped in a tunnel much as Marden had once been during the war. Marden stands up to a supreme nervous challenge, saves Dinah, and his cure becomes complete.

We may feel this to be rather a sentimental story. Most dog-stories are. But it shows a mind sensitively aware of the agony of neurotic illness precipitated by experience in battle: 'shell shock', as it was then termed. Kipling was quick to see the possibilities of occupational therapy, and the need to integrate such sufferers within a sympathetic social group. Seeking a means of achieving both these ends, he turned to Freemasonry, in which he had always been interested, and wrote several stories to illustrate how it might help, alike through the bracing effect of ritual and through practical activities. 'I cured a shell-shocker this spring by giving him our jewels to look after,' one Mason is made to report. There is no doubt something a little over-confident about this, and these stories sometimes betray an uncertainty of tone, such—we may say—as one unaccustomed to the visitation of the sick may at times exhibit. Ritual of a sort plays its part in 'The Janeites' (*Debits and Credits*), in which the members of an English battery in Flanders keep a grip on themselves by elaborating a convention of ceaseless allusive reference to Miss Austen's novels: this serves its purpose, for they hold out until the battery is destroyed and most of them are killed. 'Fairy-Kist' (*Limits and Renewals*) has some sort of irregular Masonic setting, and begins on a note of cosy dining and yarning not very happily knit to the horror of the central situation: Wollin, another war casualty, released from a mental hospital, surviving only after submission to voices which bid him wander the countryside planting flowers, involved in complex events which seem likely to result in his being convicted of murder—and finally saved by more amateur psychotherapy in which we do not quite believe.

In *Something of Myself* Kipling records what was to him, as a child, 'the loveliest sound in the world—deep-voiced men laughing together over dinner'. In his stories celebrating the mysterious power of laughter (there are plenty of them, but few seem very funny when merely summarized) women are commonly allowed a very small part. The place for laughter—significant laughter—is among men, and 'deep-voiced' men at that. Kipling's is very much a man's world, and he saw the essential masculine principle as best embodied in the ability of men to labour together to some impersonal end within the brotherhood of one or another profession, craft, or service.

Hence Kipling's unceasing need to be 'in the know' whenever the spectacle of men working together came his way. C. S. Lewis makes a shrewd observation here:

> In the last resort I do not think he loves professional brotherhood for the sake of the work; I think he loves work for the sake of professional brotherhood. . . . To belong, to be inside, to be in the know, to be snugly together against the outsiders —that is what really matters.

That this is not a wholly adequate judgement appears most clearly in those final stories in which it is the brotherhood of doctors and the work of healing which constitute the 'Inner Ring' (as Lewis calls it) to which, by an imaginative projection, Kipling seeks to 'belong'. It is very probable that as a man moves through his sixties he will have increasing personal need to consult physicians and give thought to their art. Here was no doubt the occasion of Kipling's final look at an 'Inner Ring'. But when we consider in this context Lewis's further generalization that 'the spirit of the Inner Ring is morally neutral' we may feel that it stands in need of qualification. Kipling saw great sanctity as attaching to the Hippocratic Oath, and his doctors (like his Indian Civilians, for that matter) are dedicated to purposes not reasonably to be described as 'morally neutral'. Like all men with stiff assignments, they are liable to have grown a tough skin or hard shell. But that is another matter.

'The Tender Achilles' (*Limits and Renewals*) takes its title from the legend that, when the Greek forces were being mustered for the Trojan War, the young Achilles, the future hero of the campaign, hid among women. Kipling's Achilles is Wilkett, a brilliant bacteriologist, whose work is essential to the progress of the 'Great Search' going on in the biological laboratories of St. Peggotty's Hospital. (The Great Search is Kipling's term for cancer research.) During the war Wilkett has been an army surgeon; and now, like Marden in 'The Woman in his Life', he suffers from the result of delayed shock, and breaks down. 'Everything that a man's brain automatically shoves into the background was out before the footlights,' one of his colleagues records—and goes on:

> 'Of course, I argued with him, but *you* know how much good

that is against fixed notions! I told him we were all alike, and the conditions of our job hadn't been human. I said there were limits to the machine. We'd been forced to go beyond 'em, and we ought to be thankful we'd been able to do as much as we had. Then he wrung his hands and said, "To whom much has been given, from the same much shall be required". That annoyed me. I hate book-keeping with God!'

Wilkett's breakdown results in his giving up his work and sheltering weakly with his mother. But he has a physical as well as a nervous wound, and a group of his colleagues make this the basis of a stratagem to get him back, showing him that a faulty diagnosis of his own physical trouble could not have occurred had he himself been doing his proper work. Again we may not be very impressed with the statement that an absolute cure has been achieved. But the Wilkett whose experiences in an 'S.I.W.' (hospital for self-inflicted wounds) have pushed him beyond the 'breaking strain' is convincing and moving enough.

'Unprofessional' (*Limits and Renewals*) is also about the medical profession, and takes its title from a group of research workers who go outside what their colleagues would regard as the admissible boundaries of science in their method of studying and treating cancer. The basic idea of this story relates it to 'The Eye of Allah', and more particularly to a poem entitled 'Untimely', which serves as prologue there:

> Nothing in life has been made by man for man's using
> But it was shown long since to man in ages
> Lost as the name of the maker of it. . . .

It is certain of the beliefs of mediaeval physicians that Kipling in 'Unprofessional' represents as embodying scientific truth which now has to be discovered anew. When working on 'Dayspring Mishandled' he must have read how Chaucer's Doctor of Physic

> was grounded in astronomye.
> He kepte his pacient a ful greet del
> In houres, by his magik naturel.

This means that the Doctor was careful his patients should receive their treatment at hours when the disposition of the stars was favourable. The doctors in 'Unprofessional', as a result of prolonged and lavish use of every technique known to modern science, find that their mediaeval forerunners were on the right track, since our bodily tissues prove subject to a minute but all-significant 'tidal' action arising from the motions of the stars. Thus the time of day at which a specimen of such tissues is scrutinized under the microscope may validate or invalidate a diagnosis, and compass-bearings are vital in an operating theatre. In the course of the story a woman who would otherwise have died is in fact healed by this neo-astrological medicine. There is surely something inartistic in the triumph within the fable of a therapy we know to have no existence outside it. Kipling, perhaps conscious of this, soft-pedals his conclusion. Nothing has really been achieved, one of the team says, except, perhaps, 'some data and inferences which may serve as some sort of basis for some detail of someone else's work in the future'. On this professional rather than unprofessional note the story comes to an end. Although Kipling has used all his accustomed command of detail to render the characters and their *milieu* convincing, we shall probably conclude that 'Unprofessional' is the work of a man who no longer has much impulse to elaborate 'realistic' fiction.

If this is so, it must have been deliberately that Kipling placed last in his last book of stories a companion piece to his earlier fable 'On the Gate'. 'Uncovenanted Mercies' is about the problem of pain—where pain takes the form of spiritual anguish inscrutably imposed, and inscrutably deepened and prolonged. Since hope deferred is the direst torment of all, the 'full test for Ultimate Breaking Strain' takes place in a supernal railway terminus in which men and women are made to wait through eternities for some beloved person who never turns up. It is a strangely powerful and haunting image, which may remind some readers of Kafka, and some of Sartre. But in English literature, too, there is an apposite comparison: with *The Dynasts* of Thomas Hardy. Hardy's 'Overworld', with its Spirits Sinister and Ironic, but also with its Spirit of the Pities, has some affinity with this last region of Kipling's imagining. But Kipling, once again, plucks something affirmative from the abyss. The test for ultimate breaking strain represents only Satan's carrying out the last of the tasks appointed him among the souls of the damned; and survival means that a soul has been 'reconditioned for re-issue'. *He that endureth to the end shall be saved*. This was Kipling's final reading of life.

CHAPTER TWELVE

VERSE

THE FIRST APPEARANCE of *Barrack-Room Ballads*, the basis of Kipling's reputation as a writer of verse, was in the *Scots Observer*, a literary periodical, edited by W. E. Henley, which had a high literary standard, a modest circulation, and a political leaning towards 'imperialist' policies with which Kipling's ideas fitted very well. What we have to note is that the ballads, although they were to have an enormous sale when published in book form, enjoyed their earliest acclaim within a comparatively small circle of readers possessed of a sophisticated literary taste. David Masson, an eminent professor of literature at Edinburgh and the author of a monumental life of John Milton, is said to have waved before his students a copy of Henley's paper for 22nd February 1890, and shouted: 'Here's Literature! Here's Literature at last!' He was referring to the first of the Ballads, 'Danny Deever':

> 'What are the bugles blowin' for?' said Files-on-
> Parade.
> 'To turn you out, to turn you out,' the Colour-
> Sergeant said.
> 'What makes you look so white, so white?' said
> Files-on-Parade.
> 'I'm dreadin' what I've got to watch,' the Colour-
> Sergeant said.
> For they're hangin' Danny Deever, you can hear
> the Dead March play,
> The regiment's in 'ollow square—they're
> hangin' him to-day;
> They've taken of his buttons off an' cut his
> stripes away,
> An' they're hangin' Danny Deever in the
> mornin'.

This and the three grim stanzas that follow (two of them in the same question-and-answer form) may be said to have made for Kipling the beginning of a new reputation, which was rapidly confirmed as he published poem after poem of the same general character. In how full a sense are these poems ballads?

An influential essay by T. S. Eliot provides one answer to this question. Kipling is a 'ballad-writer', Eliot says, because of a 'peculiarity of intention'. When he sometimes shows himself as a 'poet' (who is a writer of a different order in verse), this is something aside from that intention, and must be regarded simply as the involuntary manifestation of a higher power which he sometimes possessed, or which sometimes possessed him. Let us examine the argument.

Ballad verse, according to Eliot, does not represent simply a stage in the historical development of a response to poetry; on the contrary, the ballad 'corresponds to a permanent level of enjoyment of literature', and is to be found wherever the writer intends to command only a certain level of attention in his readers. To a degree unusual in one who possesses large powers of artistry and literary resource, Kipling addresses himself to the holding of this attention. He writes for the simple-minded, and seeks to convey no more than can be taken in by them in a single reading or hearing. His verse, indeed, is best when read aloud; it can then be followed easily by an untrained ear. But a true estimate of his achievement, once more, must always allow for his possession of quite exceptional talent. 'With this simplicity of purpose goes a consummate gift of word, phrase, and rhythm.' Eliot adds that the social conditions of modern society make it difficult for the good ballad to be written, but that 'Kipling had at least the inspiration and refreshment of the living music-hall'.

To this exposition something may perhaps be added from the point of view of the literary historian, for whom the ballad is, in the first instance, the 'traditional' ballad: a body of poetry anonymous in authorship, handed down through many generations only by oral transmission, and therefore often surviving in numerous versions which have come into being through variations introduced, whether consciously or unconsciously, by successive singers. In the nineteenth century this traditional ballad survived only in a few isolated communities—as, for example, in the 'Bush ballads' of Australia, or in those sung by miners and lumberjacks in certain parts of America. There were, indeed, many attempts by sophisticated writers to recover the qualities of the traditional ballad; not many are successful, since it is hard in such a form to avoid an effect of self-conscious archaism and spurious artlessness. Highly educated writers, that is to say, cannot readily produce a folk-poetry. How, then, did Kipling come to succeed?

There is another, and much more modern, type of 'popular' ballad. It is called the 'street' ballad, or 'broad-sheet' ballad. Often topically inspired, and commonly composed by writers of no great literary cultivation, it was usually printed in a form in which it could be hawked around for the custom and enjoyment of the common people. Some street ballads have great merit, but the majority are of little permanent interest. There is some affinity between the street ballad and the Music-Hall song, and we might therefore suppose that the street ballad is a significant source for Kipling. W. B. Yeats had this in mind when he described 'the grotesque tragedy of "Danny Deever" ' as exhibiting 'the matter but not the form of old street ballads'. In other words, Kipling brought an artistry of his own contriving to a sort of material—'vulgar' in the simplest sense—commonly given mediocre expression by uneducated rhymesters of little literary resource.

This, too, holds its measure of truth. Nevertheless, there remains another, and much more important, reason for Kipling's having been able to revitalize the ballad as he did. Neither Eliot nor Yeats was in a position to be much aware of it, and it has been left to Mr. Carrington to make the point. Briefly, 'barrack-room ballads' existed, and were known to Kipling, before ever he sat down to write any. And they existed under circumstances not wholly remote from those that brought the traditional ballad itself into being. ' "Danny Deever",' Mr. Carrington writes, 'is instantly recognizable by anyone who has served as a soldier . . . as actually and firmly composed in the style of the songs that the soldiers sang (and still sing) in the canteen.' Moreover, such songs, being preserved and transmitted almost exclusively by oral means, often exist in many versions. As with the traditional ballad, the songs get changed in the singing, and from this much of their vitality springs. Kipling thus had (for 'refreshment', in Eliot's phrase) this actual contact with something like true balladry behind him when he bowled over the polite readers of the *Scots Observer*.

Eliot extends the term 'ballad motive' to cover the writing of any verse in which a premium is set upon lucidity and simplicity of expression. But if we agree that a poem ceases to be essentially ballad-like when it is without a pronounced element of action or compressed narrative, it is clear that Kipling's range extends far beyond anything of the kind. It extends, for example, to something like Music-Hall song proper, in which the emphasis is upon the rapid portrayal of circumstances and character, generally in a humorous, sardonic, or (sometimes) sentimental light. The most famous example here is 'The Absent-minded Beggar', with which Kipling, it will be recalled, raised a very large relief fund at the time of the South African War:

> When you've shouted 'Rule Britannia', when you've
> sung 'God save the Queen,'
> When you've finished killing Kruger with your
> mouth,
> Will you kindly drop a shilling in my little
> tambourine
> For a gentleman in *kharki* ordered South?
> He's an absent-minded beggar, and his weaknesses
> are great—
> But we and Paul must take him as we find him—
> He is out on active service, wiping something off
> a slate—
> And he's left a lot of little things behind him!
> Duke's son—cook's son—son of a hundred kings—
> (Fifty thousand horse and foot going to Table Bay!)
> Each of 'em doing his country's work (and who's to
> look after their things?)
> Pass the hat for your credit's sake, and pay—
> pay—pay!

There is something like symbolic significance in the fact that this and its three succeeding stanzas, when set to music by the popular composer Arthur Sullivan, did so much 'to look after their things' (a term which takes for granted mistresses and illegitimate children). Kipling *used* his poetry; directed it, that is to say, to an end beyond itself. As a start, and almost for the first time in British history, he made the figure of the private soldier vivid and sympathetic. Hitherto sailors (to whom later, indeed, Kipling was to be so attracted) had held the edge over soldiers in this regard, popular sentiment always having been ready to attach itself to the navy. In the mind not only of the middle class but also of the working class from among whose failures they were largely recruited, rankers in the army were almost universally despised as brutalized and depraved—unless they were actually being killed on comfortably far-away battlefields, in which case a certain amount of patriotic feeling would be scattered over them for the time. Kipling, paradoxically, greatly raised the public image of the soldier by showing pretty faithfully that 'his weaknesses are great'. To some extent, no doubt, he is chargeable with doing this by rousing our lurking regard for tough, unscrupulous, and even brutal attitudes. A poem such as 'Loot', for example, can by no stretch of the imagination be called edifying; it represents the 'knowing' Kipling projecting himself into a seasoned soldier giving the novice tips on this topic:

> When from 'ouse to 'ouse you're 'unting, you must
> always work in pairs—
> It 'alves the gain, but safer you will find—
> For a single man gets bottled on them twisty—
> misty stairs,
> An' a woman comes and clobs 'im from be'ind.
> When you've turned 'em inside out, an' it seems
> beyond a doubt
> As if there weren't enough to dust a flute
> (*Cornet:* Toot! toot!)
> Before you sling your 'ook, at the 'ousetops take
> a look,
> For it's underneath the tiles they 'ide the loot.
> (*Chorus*) Ow the loot!
> Bloomin' loot!
> That's the thing to make the boys git up an' shoot!
> It's the same with dogs an' men,
> If you'd make 'em come again
> Clap 'em forward with a Loo! loo! Lulu! Loot!
> (*ff*) Whoopee! Tear 'im, puppy? Loo! Loo! Lulu!
> Loot! loot! loot!

In face of this astonishing performance Eliot urbanely remarks that we need not suppose Kipling to be 'commending the rapacity and greed of such irregularities, or condoning rapine'. This, of course, is true. On the other hand, it must be admitted that Kipling brings his soldiers alive for us (which must be the basis for any sympathy) in large measure by such shock tactics as these.

To make the British people aware of the realities of army life was only one step in Kipling's use of poetry. *What should they know of England who only England know?* When he produced this famous line (helped, it is said, by his mother) in 1891, it was in the first of what have been called his national odes, and the challenge was as much to his own creative powers as it was to the political thinking of his countrymen. The British Empire was various things to Kipling. First and foremost, it was a moral idea, and next after that it was an enormous storehouse of exciting and moving and fascinating sensuous impressions. It was this, much more than a mere gratifying proliferation of red patches on a map; and much more, too, than the political expression of a complex and ramifying commercial development. Kipling had, of course, an intellectual understanding of the dynamics of economic imperialism, but it was not what he kindled to. It was not what he kindled to in men like Cecil Rhodes and Theodore Roosevelt—although he knew well enough the importance of railways in Africa and coaling-stations in Cuba. To the theme of empire he brought an imagination at once historical and romantic. Upon the *Pax Romana* the *Pax Britannica* succeeds, and the true servant of either has as strong a sense of responsibility as of glory. Moreover, men in their classes and societies do not radically change, and when, in 'The Land', 'Julius Fabricus, Sub-Prefect of the Weald', gives due heed to advice on drainage offered him by 'Hobdenius—a Briton of the Clay', we are being shown something that should permanently subsist between rulers and ruled; something that Ogier the Dane, William of Warenne, and all their successors will do well to take example from. It is the historical imagination that renders Kipling (contrary to the common view of him) ultimately so tolerant to men in the diversity of their creeds and societies. He has no patience with the idea that these things can, or should, everywhere be evened out; that the uninstructed should be deferred to; that the backward and primitive should be abandoned to their own helplessness and then scorned for not running things in the fashion of Lord Beaconsfield or Mr. Gladstone. But equally he has no patience with a 'dominant' race that fails to acknowledge basic facts of human worth. 'The Ballad of East and West', composed as early as 1889, opens and closes with a statement of this:

Oh, East is East, and West is West, and never the
twain shall meet,
Till Earth and Sky stand presently at God's great
Judgement Seat;
But there is neither East nor West, Border, nor
Breed, nor Birth,
When two strong men stand face to face, though they
come from the end of the earth!

It is strange that anybody who has read the splendid ballad which is thus accompanied could go radically wrong (as many have done) in interpreting the first couplet here.

That Kipling's public vision was also romantic appears at once in another early poem, 'A Song of the English':

We were dreamers, dreaming greatly, in the man-stifled
town;
We yearned beyond the sky-line where the strange roads
go down.
Came the Whisper, came the Vision, came the Power
with the need . . .

And Rhodes himself commanded Kipling's admiration chiefly as being 'The Dreamer whose dreams come true!'. Very romantic too, but in a more popular manner, are the many poems of nostalgia (nostalgia, which can be a two-way traffic) of which the most famous, 'Mandalay', begins:

By the old Moulmein Pagoda, lookin' eastward to the sea,
There's a Burma girl a-settin', and I know she thinks
o' me;
For the wind is in the palm-trees, and the temple
bells they say:
'Come you back, you British soldier; come you back
to Mandalay!'

Come you back to Mandalay,
Where the old Flotilla lay:
Can't you 'ear their paddles chunkin' from
Rangoon to Mandalay?
On the road to Mandalay,
Where the flyin'-fishes play,
An' the dawn comes up like thunder outer
China 'crost the Bay!

We are told that Kipling composed 'Mandalay' with the air of a popular waltz in his head. Something of this sort, indeed, appears to have been his regular manner of working. He began from a tune. 'Ruddy was singing a new poem today' is an expression which Mr. Carrington tells us he has found repeatedly in Mrs. Kipling's diary.

Neither waltz tunes nor Music-Hall tunes were, of course, suitable for prompting poems of elevated national sentiment—the poems which Kipling sent straight to *The Times*, and for which he would accept no payment. But here he had another resource: that of popular hymnology. Next after the Bible itself, *Hymns Ancient and Modern* was undoubtedly the most widely diffused book throughout Victorian England. Most of the hymns themselves were such as only the most resolutely pious could admire. But everybody was familiar with their phraseology (which is biblical, in an undistinguished way) and everybody knew the tunes. To these tunes Kipling must cheerfully have sung a good deal of incongruous matter, since he certainly had them in his head when composing some of his broadest and most down-to-earth verses. But it was on the basis of these tunes, too, that he built his gravest utterances:

Land of our Birth, we pledge to thee
Our love and toil in the years to be;
When we are grown and take our place,
As men and women with our race.

Father in Heaven who lovest all,
Oh help Thy children when they call;
That they may build from age to age
An undefiled heritage. . . .

Land of our Birth, our faith, our pride,
For whose dear sake our fathers died;
Oh Motherland, we pledge to thee,
Head, heart, and hand through the years to be!

Kipling's verse does not show the same principle of development that we find, decade by decade, in his prose. This is not because it regularly fails to reflect his maturing mind—or even at times to turn 'difficult' as some of the later stories are 'difficult'. 'The Wish House', for example, is accompanied by two poems, 'Late Came the God' and 'Rahere', which at least have a fair claim to obscurity. What does not much change throughout the course of his poetry is the style, or manner of using language. To some extent this is true, too, of the prose, for at least intrusive in some of the later stories (and occasionally, indeed, pervasive in them) is a tone too jocular, cocky, knowing to be apposite and agreeable in the new context. Eliot claims that 'there is no poet who is less open to the charge of repeating himself', and this is certainly true in several regards. But what does remain a constant with Kipling is the manipulation of language in a rather flatly denotative way; as with Dryden (a comparison suggested by Eliot) the words are used to build up a powerful rhetoric, but not in that kind of subtle interaction, exploiting alike their sensuous and their associative potentialities, which distinguishes poetry proper. The explicitly national or patriotic poems are by no means the only ones dedicated to public purposes; some didactic or admonitory intention is very frequently present, and to this instrumental use of verse (having 'designs upon us', as Keats said of the less inspired Wordsworth) the development of a complex or subtle poetic would be irrelevant.

These are general statements, and all through Kipling's verse exceptions will be found. It is rather as with Dr. Johnson's friend Mr. Edwards, an aspiring philosopher upon whom, somehow, 'cheerfulness was always breaking in'. Poetry not infrequently breaks in on Kipling's verse—and as something, in Eliot's phrase, 'over and above the bargain'. It is occasionally a matter of the direct percolation of very private emotion into the work. 'The Long Trail', written in 1891, develops (as Mr. Carrington points out) complexities of rhythm which convey submerged subtleties of feeling remote from rhetorical statement.

But similar effects are to be found in the 'public' poetry. 'The Dykes' was written in 1902, after the ill-conduct of the Boer War had profoundly disturbed Kipling's sense of the security and strength of Great Britain, and when he was already more conscious than most people were of ominous forces growing on the continent of Europe. The dykes are sea-dykes. 'We were born to peace in the lee of the dykes, but the time of our peace is past.' And the poem continues:

> Far off, the full tide clambers and slips, mouthing
> and testing all,
> Nipping the flanks of the water-gates, baying along
> the wall;
> Turning the shingle, returning the shingle, changing
> the set of the sand . . .
> We are too far from the beach, men say, to know how
> the outworks stand.

This is fully imaginative. The language stirs and takes on a new power.

'The Dykes' belongs to the imperial theme, as does most of Kipling's best-known verse. But it is not in patriotic poetry that he is most original. There is plenty of such verse in English. Tennyson, who had his own xenophobic strain, had denounced the French in *In Memoriam* (a most inappropriate context) as given to 'schoolboy heat' and 'the blind hysterics of the Celt'. Tennyson, too, had exhorted his countrymen to a martial bearing through the columns of *The Times*. Swinburne had made fun of Tennyson here, but had himself in his later years vigorously exploited imperial sentiment. These and other Victorians were ahead of Kipling in the field.

It is essentially in poems not of the imperial but of the historical imagination that Kipling's finest achievement lies. The poet who comes nearest to him here is another of the Victorians, Thomas Hardy. Of the two, it is Kipling who possesses in the higher degree one crucial endowment—one already remarked upon in this study. It is a sense of the past that is deeply intuitive, approximating almost to a kind of clairvoyance, as if at some deep level of his mind there existed an abnormal freedom from the stricter boundaries of time and place. Eliot speaks of him as 'almost "possessed" of a kind of second sight'—and indeed returns to this thought in his main summary of Kipling's powers:

> Kipling, apparently merely the reflection of the world about him, is the most inscrutable of authors. An immense gift for using words, an amazing curiosity and power of observation with his mind and with all his senses, the mask of the entertainer, and beyond that a queer gift of second sight, of transmitting messages from elsewhere, a gift so disconcerting when we are made aware of it that thenceforth we are never sure when it is *not* present: all this makes Kipling a writer impossible wholly to understand and quite impossible to belittle.

There is another insistence in Eliot's essay: that we must finally judge Kipling 'not separately as a poet and as a writer of prose fiction, but as the inventor of a mixed form'. It is true that Kipling came with increasing regularity to accompany his stories sometimes with a verse prologue, and sometimes with both a prologue and epilogue. The effect is not always felicitous; and when there is failure it is generally because the imagination at work in the story has been operating at a deeper level than the imagination operating in the poem or poems. We have noticed an example in the verses prefacing 'They'. There is a more striking instance in those set at the end of 'Mary Postgate', in which we are told that the English had 'long arrears to make good' when at length they 'began to hate'. This is no doubt congruous with the surface of the story, but may distort it for us when we are trying to view it in depth.

It is in *Puck of Pook's Hill* and *Rewards and Fairies* that there is often something like perfect command of the 'mixed form', prose and verse alike celebrating the historical continuity of the English consciousness, as Kipling saw it. It is a consciousness forged out of history—and in a sense out of geography too, since the land itself had gone to the making of that consciousness as it passes, within these islands, from race to race.

At the beginning of his great story, *Heart of Darkness*, Joseph Conrad sketches what he supposes might be the effect upon some young Roman legionary of being quartered in 'one of the dark places of the earth': Britain in the first century of our era:

He has to live in the midst of the incomprehensible, which is also detestable. And it has a fascination, too, that goes to work upon him. The fascination of the abomination—you know, imagine the growing regrets, the longing to escape, the powerless disgust, the surrender, the hate.

Kipling's vision of Britain begins as early as this—

And see you, after rain, the trace
Of mound and ditch and wall?
O that was a Legion's camping-place,
When Caesar sailed from Gaul—

yet his Romans feel themselves to belong to the country upon which they have set the stamp of civilization; hence the Song of the Centurion ordered back to Rome in A.D. 300:

I've served in Britain forty years, from Vectis to
the Wall.
I have none other home than this, nor any life at all.
Last night I did not understand, but, now the hour
draws near
That calls me to my native land, I feel that land is here.

For Kipling, too, this civilization, although always under threat (as 'A Pict Song' tells), is yet never wholly breached; and its defence and furtherance is the one task that matters. We shall succeed only if we learn to feel and understand and reverence the past as entering constantly into the present, bearing fortitude, wisdom, richness of experience in its hands. The poems in these books, although so variously mooded and conceived, tend to centre upon this great theme of historical continuity. The finest of them add something more: an elegiac note. 'Cities and Thrones and Powers' has this note, and so has 'The Way through the Woods':

They shut the road through the woods
Seventy years ago.
Weather and rain have undone it again,
And now you would never know
There was once a road through the woods

Before they planted the trees.
It is underneath the coppice and heath
And the thin anemones.
Only the keeper sees
That, where the ring-dove broods,
And the badgers roll at ease,
There was once a road through the woods.

Yet, if you enter the woods
Of a summer evening late,
When the night-air cools on the trout-ringed pools
Where the otter whistles his mate,
(They fear not men in the woods,
Because they see so few)
You will hear the beat of a horse's feet,
And the swish of a skirt in the dew,
Steadily cantering through
The misty solitudes,
As though they perfectly knew
The old lost road through the woods . . .
But there is no road through the woods.

CONCLUSION

LIMITS AND RENEWALS, published in 1932, was Kipling's last volume of stories. It received little notice, and even the majority of his admirers seem to have regarded it as the work of an ageing and tired man. This was to do injustice to the book. It is true that its title—carefully chosen, as all Kipling's titles were—can be felt as carrying a reference not merely to the limits of human endurance in general but also to something which Kipling now feels true of himself. But the renewals are as important as the limits. Minds, like bodies, can be healed; and, as we have seen, the best stories in the book show Kipling's imagination as rekindled before this theme.

His own physical health was much impaired, and he suffered a great deal of pain from causes which his doctors failed effectively to diagnose. It seems probable, too, that round this affliction there grew up a further burden of morbid anxieties. His life at Bateman's was sheltered, and indeed enclosed. It may even have been injudiciously over-protected. The novelist Hugh Walpole described Mrs. Kipling as 'a good strong-minded woman, who has played watch-dog to him so long that she knows just how to save him any kind of disturbance, mental, physical, or spiritual'. We may think it possible that Kipling would have benefited from rather less of this, and from maintaining more contact with the practical concerns of life. But this can be no more than speculation. There was a good deal of hospitality at Bateman's, to which relations brought their children, in whose company Kipling delighted; and he continued to take pleasure in short cruises, and in motor tours—particularly through France, the only foreign country for which he never betrayed other than a warm regard.

Nevertheless, Kipling's isolation increased with the years. During the period when he was compiling *The Irish Guards in the Great War* he had seen a good deal of young soldiers who had been contemporaries of his son, but after that his acquaintance was confined, in the main, to contemporaries of his own. They tended to be men of eminence—although not of the first eminence—in the public life of the country, and he appears to have had little patience with anybody not of his own ultra-conservative way of thinking. His correspondence with Rider Haggard, from at least 1918 until Haggard's death in 1925, is pervasively pessimistic in tone. Sometimes he arraigns the human situation at large, declaring his certainty that this world has every attribute of a hell, and that he has an active faith in the existence of a personal devil. More commonly his despondency is occasioned by the state of the Empire. Australia is 'an unchaste and idle democracy'. India is being given away, and no white woman should visit or remain there. The state of affairs in Ireland and Egypt is equally bad; in fact Britain's whole tremendous achievement is being let fall to pieces. He spends a few days in Holland, and finds the Dutch 'manufacturing arms for the Hun's next war, and enjoying enormous and expensive prosperity'; even the aeroplanes there are 'being tried out for the Boches'. Kipling was not to live to see the destruction of Rotterdam by the *Luftwaffe*.

At home, too, Kipling was at loggerheads with almost every trend of government. He believed his cousin Stanley Baldwin, now leader of the Conservative Party, to be 'reasonably sincere and honest'; Stan was pretty well a Socialist at heart, all the same. Along with Haggard, Kipling became prominent on a body to be known as the Liberty League, which was to develop 'a mighty plan for fighting Bolshevism in this country, by means of elaborate propaganda'; unfortunately one of the founders of the League developed a small plan strictly in terms of private enterprise, and the League faded out when its funds vanished. He came to believe in the machinations of the Jews and the dangerousness of the Trade Unions. When Philip Kerr, later Marquess of Lothian, was appointed a Rhodes Trustee, Kipling at once resigned his own Trusteeship, publicly declining to serve with an internationalist and a Liberal. 'Let me hear you cuss the present state of things,' one of his letters to Haggard concludes. 'I'm run out of comminations for the moment.'

Some at least of Kipling's forebodings were justified. Like Winston Churchill (whom he never forgave for a speech directed against Lord Milner in 1906) he was early conscious of the menace of Nazi Germany. One of the most impressive of his later poems, 'The Storm Cone', written in 1932, is prophetic enough:

This is the midnight—let no star
Delude us—dawn is very far.
This is the tempest long foretold—
Slow to make head but sure to hold.

Stand by! The lull 'twixt blast and blast
Signals the storm is near, not past;
And worse than present jeopardy
May our forlorn to-morrow be . . .

Kipling's death in January 1936 was immediately followed by that of King George V, and it thus came about that, within a few days of each other, services were held in Westminster Abbey both for the Head of the British Empire and for the great writer whom the imperial theme had inspired. Kipling's burial in the Abbey was a high honour paid to his genius; the last writer to be buried there had been Thomas Hardy, in 1928. Hardy's pall-bearers included James Barrie, John Galsworthy, Edmund Gosse, A. E. Housman, Bernard Shaw, and Rudyard Kipling himself. Kipling's pall-bearers, like Hardy's, were led by the Prime Minister, but no members of the craft of letters came behind. An Admiral, a General, a representative of the War Graves Commission, the Master of a Cambridge College, a cousin, and two old friends: whether fitly or unfitly, it was these who bore Kipling's ashes to Poets' Corner in the south transept.

PRINCIPAL PUBLICATIONS REFERRED TO

1888 *Plain Tales from the Hills* (Thacker, Spink & Co., Calcutta)
1888 *Soldiers Three* (Pioneer Press, Allahabad)
1888 *In Black and White* (A. H. Wheeler & Co., Allahabad)
1888 *The Phantom Rickshaw* (A. H. Wheeler & Co., Allahabad)
1888 *Wee Willie Winkie* (A. H. Wheeler & Co., Allahabad)
1891 *The Light that Failed* (Macmillan & Co.)
1891 *Life's Handicap* (Macmillan & Co.)
1892 *The Naulahka* (William Heinemann)
1893 *Many Inventions* (Macmillan & Co.)
1894 *The Jungle Book* (Macmillan & Co.)
1895 *The Second Jungle Book* (Macmillan & Co.)
1897 *Captains Courageous* (Macmillan & Co.)
1898 *The Day's Work* (Macmillan & Co.)
1899 *Stalky & Co.* (Macmillan & Co.)
1901 *Kim* (Macmillan & Co.)
1902 *Just-so Stories* (Macmillan & Co.)
1904 *Traffics and Discoveries* (Macmillan & Co.)
1906 *Puck of Pook's Hill* (Macmillan & Co.)
1909 *Actions and Reactions* (Macmillan & Co.)
1910 *Rewards and Fairies* (Macmillan & Co.)
1917 *A Diversity of Creatures* (Macmillan & Co.)
1926 *Debits and Credits* (Macmillan & Co.)
1932 *Limits and Renewals* (Macmillan & Co.)
1937 *Something of Myself* (Macmillan & Co.)
1940 *Verse: Definitive Edition* (Hodder and Stoughton)